PRAISE FOR STORIES OF RESISTANCE

"We, in early childhood education, understand the power of storytelling and in this book, the authors use that power to tell their stories, stories so familiar to many of us, of overcoming odds and challenges to victory and success. Iyanla Vanzant says, "It's important that we share our experiences with other people. Your story will heal you and your story will heal somebody else. When you tell your story, you free yourself and give other people permission to acknowledge their own story." This book will do just that—encourage and support others to tell their stories and move towards healing, and celebration. These women are not asking for a seat at the table—that implies someone else's ownership of the table—they are building a table and inviting us all to it."

—Ann McClain Terrell, NAEYC Governing Board Past President and Author, *Graceful Leadership in Early Childhood Education*

"Seats at the decision making table can be quite seductive—cause one to lose one's head. The search for answers to the questions, How did it happen? Why am I here? can be unsettling. The personal stories of the Black women contributing to *Stories of Resistance* offer powerful rationales for the "hows and whys." The seat(s) are for those committed to operationalizing "what ought to be"—a place where equity and social justice prevail as the default mode. The seat's power is situational depending heavily on its occupant; she who is unapologetically centered at the apex of her cultural intersections; she who is propelled by an urgency to find and with a high degree of intentionality make her voice heard. Her seat moves with her!"

—Jerlean Daniel, Ph.D.
Former Executive Director, National Association for the Education of Young Children (NAEYC)

"Bless you, Alissa for taking to heart Toni Morrison's words: "If there is a book that you want to read, but it hasn't been written yet, then you must write it." This is the book YOU wanted to read growing up, and I suspect that is true for many, many Black women. This is a book we all must read because it affirms Blackness yet shatters any single idea about what it means to be Black; because Alissa introduces us to provocative, diverse and inspiring stories of Black women in the early childhood profession, reminding us these stories are likely all around us in any job setting, in most organizations and communities.

Here is an authentic offering to learn from 12 Black women in Early Care and Education. Whether you read this book as an assignment, or something you came upon, you'll discover gems and wonderings, maybe delighting in the comfort of something familiar, or the gift of a perspective you hadn't yet appreciated. You'll find you want to share lessons from this book in the many settings of your life, perhaps including new self-awareness, perhaps suggesting forming a study-for-action together."

—Margie Carter
Early Childhood author, thinking partner, and consultant

"Much appreciation to Alissa Mwenelupembe and the other brave women who have shared their poignant stories for this important book. It is long past time for leaders of color with strong voices, powerful stories and new thinking to be heard. Their stories call out, push back and transcend the white centered perspectives and power structures that have dominated the field of early childhood for too long. Along with the compelling content, this book is beautifully designed with inspirational words, quotes and photos of the courageous women who are featured. We have much to learn from this book as we decenter whiteness and transform our profession."

—Deb Curtis
Toddler and Adult Educator, Author

STORIES OF RESISTANCE

LEARNING FROM BLACK WOMEN IN EARLY CARE AND EDUCATION

COLLECTED BY ALISSA MWENELUPEMBE

Exchange Press

ISBN 978-0-942702-82-8
eISBN 978-0-942702-83-5

© 2023 Alissa Mwenelupembe

Book Design: Chelsea Parker
Editor: Erin Glenn

This book may not be reproduced in whole or in part by any means without written permission of the publisher.

For more information about other Exchange Press publications and resources for directors and teachers, contact:

Exchange Press
7700 A Street
Lincoln, NE 68510
(800) 221-2864
ExchangePress.com

DEDICATION

To Maya:
your bold spirit
inspires me
to always stretch
a little farther
than I feel comfortable
so that I can stay
just a few steps
ahead of you
to light your path.
I am confident
that you will
move mountains.

ACKNOWLEDGEMENTS

This book is about a community and I could not have pulled it off without so many amazing women. First, I want to thank the women who contributed their essays. Kelly, Meghan, Jerletha, Theressa, Joyce, Nadiyah, Crystal, Rukia, Cynthia, Olga, and Brandy—thank you for sharing your story. The amount of vulnerability this act of writing required was extraordinary and I am grateful that each of you agreed to go there with me. Thanks to Sara Gilliam who spent weeks editing the manuscript with me to make it ready for publication. Thank you to the team at Exchange Press—Erin, Scott, and Chelsea—our calls were always so joyful and you made this process feel much easier than it probably was. Thank you to the Black women in my life that do not show up in this book. Your stories are woven into the tapestry of all of our stories. And a final thank you to my husband Sekela who always supports my big ideas and helps provide the space and support for me to shine bright.

TABLE OF CONTENTS

5	Introduction
10	Rooted: Theressa Lenear
26	Authentic: Jerletha Mcdonald
34	Defining: Cynthia Davis-Vanloo
52	Determined: Joyce Jackson
62	Limitless: Nadiyah Taylor
74	Reassurance: Brandy James
82	Passion: Rukia Rogers
92	Rebirth: Crystal Sanford-Brown
108	Intersectionality: Meghan L. Green
120	Resolute: Olga Lacayo
136	Planted: Kelly Ramsey
152	Resilience: Alissa Mwenelupembe
160	Afterword

"BECAUSE I HAD FIGURED OUT HOW TO GET MY SEAT AT THE TABLE ... IT WAS MY RESPONSIBILITY TO HELP OTHERS FIND THEIRS."

— ALISSA MWENELUPEMBE

INTRODUCTION

Right after college, I worked in the reception area of a doctor's office for a large clinic that had offices all over the city. I spent my training working in various offices, from family practice to pediatrics. When my training was complete, I found myself working for a pulmonologist and an allergist. I never actually encountered the physicians in my short time there, just the nurses. The nurse for the pulmonologist was kind of a loud white lady. She seemed difficult and hard to please, but even though I was young, I already knew that people were like that sometimes. The other people at the front desk were quiet and I wasn't connecting well with them either. I spent a lot of time missing my previous coworkers from the pediatricians' office, who liked to joke and have fun while they worked.

One day, my boss, Connie, called me into her office. I really didn't have any idea what the problem was. She told me that the nurse that I was struggling with had come to her and reported me for being rude. The nurse told her that I yelled at her and put my finger in her face.

I was shocked. That had never happened. I was a fairly mousy, quiet girl and would never dream of doing that to someone at work. Connie assured me that she didn't think that was something I would do, either. But then she said that she noticed I talk with my hands a lot, and the nurse probably misunderstood me. My heart sank even further. I had barely even talked to this nurse at all. I tried to avoid her. I was too timid to say it, but I knew. That nurse had a problem with me because I was Black. She expected me to be a certain way because of her own biases about Black women. When I left Connie's office that day, I knew I wasn't going to be working there long, and a couple of weeks later I quit with no notice.

That nurse resurfaced in another body years later, after I had gotten into early childhood education. I was living in a new city, and through some mutual friends I had the opportunity to meet Margie Carter and Deb Curtis, authors and leaders in early childhood education. Margie became my pen pal. I wrote to her when I was struggling to figure out how to lead my staff, and she always gave me sage advice. Each time she and Deb came back to our city, I was able to engage with them further, and as time went on, I also included my staff. I was a part of a network of other programs that were working to improve their quality. I was the new kid on the block, and the rest of the directors were native to the city and had been in the network for a while. I had grown very fond of all of them and I knew that they could benefit from the connection I had created with Margie as well.

I began trying to make connections, first through the coach who worked with my program and then higher up. I really wanted to see everyone have the opportunities I was gaining access to. But, "Nurse 2.0," the leader of the project that housed our network of programs, had other ideas. I was told that

> "SOMEHOW, I TOOK THESE EXPERIENCES AND MANY MORE AND I USED THEM TO MAKE ME STRONG."
>
> — ALISSA MWENELUPEMBE

I was opportunistic and needed to stay in my lane. My attempts to engage in dialogue around our work were viewed as me being a troublemaker. Once again, I looked around the table I was sitting at and saw white faces looking back at me. I was being told without words that I needed to learn my place. I didn't last too much longer in that program. I got to the point where I felt like I was hurting my program by not backing down and falling in line. I put my tail between my legs and moved back to my hometown.

I wish I could say that was the first or the last time that the color of my skin has led to me being treated differently, but I can't. That one experience is just a story in a collection of stories that I could share. This experience is one that still sits with me. I think about it when I meet someone new, when I interview for a job, when I meet my children's teachers, or when I go through the checkout line in the grocery store. I wonder, "Will this person think I'm an 'angry Black woman' if I complain about something that wasn't right?" "Will my future employer take me seriously?" "How can I share what I do for a living with my children's teachers, so they know I am serious about their education?" Walking through the world while Black is simultaneously proving you are competent and nonthreatening, that you could do someone's job, but that you aren't trying to take it.

Somehow, I took these experiences and many more and I used them to make me strong. My experiences have been the stepping stones that have helped me cross to the other side of the river. Sometimes, other people have given me a stone along the way. I leave these stones for the women who come after me, and I return from time to time to make sure they are still visible.

Sometimes, I return and stones have washed away, so I add new ones. Other times, the river current has picked up and a few more stones are needed for safety. Right now, the river is traveling so fast that I had to gather a group of women who have stones of their own and add them to the path. In our professional world, these stones in the river are seats at the table.

A couple of years ago, I sat with my friend and colleague, Kelly Ramsey, in the convention center at a conference hosted by NAEYC. I was there as a governing board member; she was a presenter. Between the two of us we had led organizations, written articles, managed teams, and found our way into leadership roles. I asked Kelly, "How did we get here?"

By design, we should not have found ourselves in the spaces in which we were sitting. I had grown up poor; an average student in a family where I was the first to attend college. I hadn't even planned to work in this field, but it found me and I thrived. Kelly thought for a moment and said something that laid the groundwork for a new course in my life. She said that even though we weren't always invited to the table, we kept showing up, often carrying our own seats. That day, I realized that because I had figured out how to get my seat at the table (even if it meant bringing my own), it was my responsibility to help others find theirs.

This book is filled with stories of women who found their seats at the table. In addition to sharing their story, I also asked each author to choose one word that they feel best describes their journey. Each essay begins with that word. Keep that word in mind while you read, and reflect on its meaning.

As you read these stories, I also encourage you to take time to reflect on how they might mirror your own experiences or how they might feel very foreign to you. After each story, I invite you to delve deeper with reflection questions.

While all of the stories are very different, common threads run through each of them. These threads create a tapestry that reflects the experiences of Black women in America. The women who wrote these stories come from different backgrounds and walks of life. Some have written and published articles and books, while others are writing for the very first time. As you read their stories, I hope you can hear their voices as my goal was to preserve each unique voice and to keep the stories as authentic and real as possible. It is my hope that you find inspiration in these stories that you can take into your own life. And that some of you, who maybe already have seats at the table, might move over and make room for a new person to join you.

—Alissa Mwenelupembe

"I AM FROM THE POWER OF THOSE WHO CAME BEFORE, WHO ERASE MY DOUBTS OF MY EXISTANCE, WHO FUEL MY RESISTANCE, AND WHO GUIDE ME IN CREATING GIFTS OF LOVE FOR THE FUTURE."

— THERESSA LENEAR

ROOTED
THERESSA LENEAR

Where I'm From

I am from the elements unknown as to my beginning
but appears to be the sharecropper connected to the "rez"
and the peoples of greatness who inhabited this land
before Columbus made his so-called discovery.

I am from the peoples of greatness from the place
where all people kind sprung forth
only to be stolen and forced to build this country
under the heavy blanket of enslavement.
I am from the mixture of tastes of fried eggs and bacon
encased in buttery grits swirling around in my mouth.

THERESSA LENEAR

I am from the bright red, blue, green and yellow lights
dancing magically across the dark sky
hovering over the crisp white glistening powder
as it lays upon the frozen land and in the summer,
the sun shining brightly at midnight.

I am from the "Dominus vobiscum, et cum spiritu tuo" and
"Father, bless me for I have sinned,"
feeding my brain and soul with the knowledge
that evokes – "you are a credit to your race" mentality.

I am from "where do I come from?" pulling me in all directions
while six life lines keep me grounded in motherhood;
the fourteen verses contributing to the song of grand motherhood;
and now the heartbeats of five that grant me great grand motherhood.

I am from the power of those who came before,
who erase my doubts of my existence, who fuel my resistance,
and who guide me in creating gifts of love for the future.

— Theressa Lenear (revised 2020, 2018, 2015, 2012)

A STORY, MY STORY

I began my master's thesis, "Umoja–The Unity That Brings Us Together" (1999):

> *"I think and I feel that it is important to hear the stories. For in the stories are the histories of the people, their struggles and their triumphs, their resistance and their oppression, their battles won and their battles lost. Within their stories lay the answers to many of life's questions. Their journeys provide pathways to follow and pathways to avoid. But before I can truly listen and hear their stories, I must listen to my own story. In hearing my story, I gain the clarity of self and can see the paths taken to reach the person that I am today. It is important to me, as a person of color, to pass on to others the wisdom of the seasons of life, the lessons I have learned and the knowledge I have gained."*

So, we begin a story. My story.

I was born in Bremerton, Washington on October 20, 1943. My mother had a great story about her pregnancy and my subsequent birth; mama was a great storyteller. My mother was born on a reservation in Idaho. Her mom was of mixed race, but met the blood quantum to be registered in the Blackfoot tribe; her dad was a Merchant Marine from the French Barbados Island. When she was young, her large family moved to Eastern Washington and were migrant farmworkers. She told many stories about her experiences.

My father also came from a large family, which originally migrated from Alabama to Louisiana and were sharecroppers. My father had a beautiful voice; he sounded like Brook Benton and really wanted to be in the entertainment world. Unfortunately for him, his father, being a minister, frowned upon such a vocation as being "in the life of the devil." As soon as he was old enough, my father moved north and joined the military. He served in a segregated military and was discharged from service after he struck his commanding officer for calling him "boy." This was not the first, nor the only time, that word and others fell upon my father's ears. There comes a point where one is tired of walking away.

> "THERE COMES A POINT WHERE ONE IS TIRED OF WALKING AWAY."
>
> — THERESSA LENEAR

The United States purchased the Alaska Territory from Russia in 1867, with the intent of mutual benefit for both parties. Gold was discovered and with World War II, many men headed north to Alaska to search for gold and construction work that was available with the building of the railroad and the Alaskan Highway. My father left in search of work, and my mother and I followed by ferry a few months later; I was a little over two years old.

We moved to Fairbanks after living a year in Juneau. Fairbanks was and is considered the "golden heart" of Alaska, and when we moved there, it was a small pioneer town and the gateway to finding gold in the streams and the mountains. My physical presence was newsworthy, as there was an article announcing to the town that Theressa Lee Coleman, daughter of Beatrice and Robert R. Coleman, was the first colored child living in their town. The dearth of "colored" families and children living in the Fairbanks area created a mirror, in which I saw all children—white, negro, and Alaska native—looking similar in the wintertime. In the coldest months, children were all snuggled and bundled up in their winter clothing, through which only a small part of their faces was visible. In the summertime, everyone's skin reflected different shades of brown as the children tanned under the long summer sun-filled days and nights.

The majority of the population was Alaskan native peoples of several nations (Haida, Tlingit, Aleuts, Athabaskan, Eskimo, and Tsimshian), who were living off the land as their ancestors had done for decades. The dominant white cultural influence and its so-called civilization, which was imposed upon these native people, was reflected in rates of disease, alcoholism, the raping of the land's wealth, the missionaries' diligence in saving these poor "savages'" souls from damnation and, yes, in racism.

We lived in a cabin until my father built our house. I went moose and caribou hunting with him every fall. We ate lots of salmon, wild rabbits, bear, and buffalo. My mother planted a huge garden every summer—my sister and I had to do the weeding—and she canned vegetables and made jellies with the fall berries we collected. Being part native provided my mother a place at the table with the other indigenous women, where she had the honor to learn to use seal skin when making our parkas and mukluks, along with beautiful beadwork.

THERESSA LENEAR

Fast forward. In 1969, I was homeless with three small children. It was the Vietnam War era, and my husband fled to Canada while we were visiting his family in Chicago, leaving the children and me to fend for ourselves. My firstborn was enrolled in a summer Head Start program, and as the door of my marriage closed, the door of opportunity opened when I returned home to Alaska. I took a position as a parent aide at that Head Start program, working with three-year-olds; it was a far cry from the age group I was intending to teach—middle schoolers.

I blossomed and flourished within this environment. I took classes in early childhood education and moved from parent aide to teacher assistant to teacher, and finally to master teacher. I loved how involved families were in their children's care and education. This held me accountable for providing the best nurturing learning environment, where all felt visible, valued, and validated. My code of ethics was the values and morals that my parents instilled in me: be humble, keep your word, have integrity, be honest, and practice what you preach! I strove to be a reflective practitioner, continually assessing areas of personal growth and creating skills and abilities that would benefit the children, families, and communities I served.

I was able to get my two-year degree in between giving birth to two more children. With the birth of my sixth child, I decided to stay at home, and I became a licensed family child care provider. On the brink of a second divorce, I felt like a complete failure; I sank into depression. My sense of self and the related confidence was flushed away when my husband walked out of our marriage.

ROOTED

My mother passed away a few months later. My economic situation now required me to become gainfully employed, in order to support my family, but the employment I secured was not working in a community of young children and their families. My world was topsy-turvy. My children were the light at the end of the tunnel. They drew me out of my funk and down the path of self-discovery. From this process of metamorphosis, I emerged a beautiful butterfly.

In 1986, I made a life-changing decision to move to Seattle, Washington. I left Fairbanks behind with encouragement from my friends and the doubts of my ex-husband that I could make it on my own. I drove through a blizzard in the mountain pass in the dark of night to reach Haines Junction. From there, I took the ferry through the inside water passage and arrived in Seattle on Halloween, 1987. The trip had a symbolic meaning for me, as it was completing the circle. I was returning to the home of my birth in the same manner that I had left. I was to begin a new life after living in Alaska for more than forty years. I was home. I had come full circle.

When I reflect on my personal and professional life, I can see that there was a design and purpose in the journey that followed that deepened my development of self. I have found that nothing happens by chance, as there are always opportunities where one can self-reflect on lessons learned. My experience with racism in Alaska was direct and overt, while what I experienced in the Pacific Northwest was hidden and covert. There were several opportunities that provided me with a frame to build upon my own self-development and further the work that I would do within different communities. I forged authentic relationships with others in the field, and sought out and created strong networks that moved the agenda to positively impact the quality of services and resources designated for children, families, and communities. The work that I did was in support of all children and their families, particularly children and families of color.

> "THE DOOR OPENED AND BECKONED ME TO ENTER."
>
> — THERESSA LENEAR

I got a position at a co-op program in Seattle's University District, where I was the lead teacher of a classroom of early three-year-old children. Many of their parents or family representatives volunteered in the classroom as assistants. I loved this, as it was so similar to the work I had done with the Head Start program in Fairbanks. One of my parents was a student at Pacific Oaks College. She was unable to attend a class that weekend and encouraged me to go in her place.

The door opened and beckoned me to enter. That weekend, I found myself in the company of a diverse group of people who became close friends, colleagues, and allies. That weekend, I experienced engaging with my first instructor of color. I talked openly about issues that impacted me as a woman of color with others, both people of color and European Americans. The world shifted.

It was during this time (1990) that I became a part of a group of African American professionals concerned about the quality of care and education and access to resources for African American children and their families. We wanted to create change. The process for empowerment and leadership development, which resulted from our collective efforts, enabled the group to

"I ALWAYS BRING WHO I AM,
AS A CULTURAL BEING, AND
NEGOTIATE WITHIN THAT CONTEXT."

— THERESSA LENEAR

co-author and publish with funding from the National Black Child Development Institute, the results from our research project and the implementation of the action agenda items.

We still meet monthly, and are engaged in issues impacting African American children and families. Our collective effort was a model for other culturally-specific communities to come together and engage in a similar process, and subsequently publish their findings and action agendas on behalf of their communities. At different times, the groups received funding from state, county, and city systems, in order to implement their action agenda items.

Around this time, Louise Derman-Sparks was developing a three-year research project on Anti-Bias Education Leadership, with three sites. I and several of my colleagues applied to participate, and were selected for the Seattle site. From this project, opportunities arose for us to explore and investigate our cultural histories and work with diverse communities and programs around culturally relevant and anti-bias issues.

Not long after (1992), I became the director of special projects at Child Care Resources, through which we had received grant funding for a systems integration project. I noticed something about the conversations on systems integration—we were not engaging in the institutional constructs that were impacting the quality of life for our children, families, and communities. Instead, the system seemed to blame the victims and overlook or diminish these individual acts of discrimination and bias.

ROOTED

I was tired of this framing of our experiences. While attending the National Association for the Education of Young Children Conference in New Orleans, a reception was hosted by the People's Institute for Survival and Beyond, a national training organization. I had researched the organization, and I invited the training team to come to King County and provide trainings for one hundred people addressing "undoing racism," as this was impacting the quality of life in our community. I was tired of "talking nice" and wanted those of us touching the lives of children and families to get real. What is racism and how can we undo it? What role did we play? The People's Institute's theory is that racism has been systematically constructed, and therefore can be deconstructed by understanding the history from which racism comes, how racism works, how and why racism is kept in place, and the interdependence of racism and classism. We learned strategies for organizing to change the dynamics as our county took on the challenge.

The opportunity to complete my bachelor's and master's degrees at Pacific Oaks College, as part of a cohort of students of color, came at the most opportune and appropriate time. This cohort allowed all of us to build upon and nurture our sense of self, our confidence and our competence, while going through a higher learning institution within a system that historically and traditionally did not support students of color. I wrote a paper reflecting on my experience titled, "Rocky Road, and I Don't Mean the Flavor: A Student's Reflection." In it I wrote,

> "It was a beautiful warm sunny day and I was nervous, very nervous. As I stepped from my car, I told myself to breathe—

breathe deep, deep breaths. More and more cars were pulling up to the curb and parking, with the people then exiting their vehicles and entering the school's gymnasium.

'I did it Mom,' I said as I looked up towards the sky. It was June 12th, 1999. The Pacific Oaks College Northwest Graduation celebration. I and others had completed our various program requirements and now with our families, friends, community members, allies, and peers present, we were preparing to receive our official rewards for the fruits of our labor."

I delivered a speech that day on behalf of the master's students. My six children were present in the audience and I placed my gaze upon them as I spoke. At the age of fifty-six, I officially received my degree, a master of arts in human development with a specialization in bicultural development.

When I reflect on my journey during that specific time and space, I can see the stepping stones that fueled me, propelled me, and held me accountable to the work that must be done.

1. The claiming of who I am and development of my own cultural identity. Having the clarity of who I am as a woman of color moved me to what Antonia Darder calls "cultural negotiation." I am bicultural, and I know how to navigate within the dominant society. I know the rules of the game and can speak the language. I always bring who I am as a cultural being, and negotiate within that context.

2. The finding of my voice as a confident and competent professional. Even as an extreme introvert, my confidence in my knowledge and expertise moves me to speak on issues I find meaningful and essential.

3. My participation in collective efforts for social change. Engaging in collaborative efforts in organizing keeps the issues up front and visible.

These have created within me more of a thirst for knowledge and desire to expand on these areas. As an elder who just turned seventy-seven, I know and understand that I am a lifelong learner. My window is wide open, so bring it on!

THERESSA LENEAR

Theressa Lenear has over fifty-four years of experience in the early childhood education field. She has worked with many young children in multiple settings in both Alaska and Washington. Her focus centers on teaching, mentoring, and coaching adults wishing to strengthen their skills in providing services and resources relevant to the diverse children and families in their communities.

She is a faculty member at Goddard College in the graduate program and working in her community is a cultural expectation and a collective responsibility. Theressa co-leads the Teaching Umoja Participatory Action Research Commitment in examining ethnic identity, bicultural, cross-cultural, and triliteracy development of children of color. This work is a collaborative effort with diverse co-researchers from across the United States and the communities of Port Royal and Moore Town, Jamaica. Theressa is actively engaged with others working on issues of equity and social justice.

REFLECTION QUESTIONS

1 Theressa describes a childhood in Alaska where she was the minority, yet seemed to be celebrated as new and unique. How was her experience among Alaskan natives similar and different from the experiences many Black and brown children have living in communities that do not reflect them?

2 Even though she faced hardships, Theressa was able to do extraordinary things, and her list of accomplishments is long. What role did her connection to early childhood education (Head Start in particular) play in her success?

3 Theressa mentions that she graduated in a cohort from Pacific Oaks College that was composed of all students of color. Why do you think that such a cohort existed? What benefits might students of color receive from being in a group like that?

4 Theressa describes the stepping stones that "fueled her, propelled her, and held her accountable to the work that must be done." Reflect on some stepping stones in your own life.

"ONE MUST BE COMPLETELY FOCUSED ON THE GOAL AHEAD AND PROCEED UNAPOLOGETICALLY IN BOLDNESS."

— JERLETHA MCDONALD

AUTHENTIC
JERLETHA MCDONALD

"A leader sees greatness in other people. He nor she can be much of a leader if all she sees is herself." — Maya Angelou

As a young African American girl, I learned the definition of leadership and the action it demands at an early age. I was raised by my grandmother, along with my brother and five cousins in Northern California. My mother experienced various disparities, which left my grandmother to provide care for me and my brother.

My grandmother was a strong, God-fearing woman. She was a pillar in her community, well-respected, and determined to make the best of what she had. She radiated a sense of security and stability that was soothing to everyone who met her. She provided a safe haven for us and worked hard to assure that we were all protected. I would often stare at her in admiration as I witnessed how she would always make a way in the most difficult of times. She had become my example, and in my heart I wanted to emulate her greatness. Because of her, I knew I must choose greater endeavors.

At the age of six, I was much taller than the other first graders in my class. I yearned to be shorter, and often would slump down when lining up for class to create a false equality to my classmates' height.

"Why can't I be shorter?" I often questioned myself. I felt that my height was abnormal and I stuck out like a sore thumb amongst the other children in my class. One day after school, I decided to confide my feelings to my grandmother.

"I'm too tall," I wailed, as tears poured down my face.

"What do you mean you're too tall?" my grandmother asked.

"I'm the tallest girl in my class! The other first graders are shorter than me!"

My grandmother's eyes gazed into mine as she shifted her focus to a magazine that was placed near her.

"Do you see this lady, Jerletha? She is tall and beautiful like you, and look! She is on the cover of a magazine! Her name is Naomi Campbell."

As I gazed at the picture of the model, I began to feel a resolve that stopped my weeping.

"One day this will be you," my grandmother exclaimed. "You must walk in your greatness! Don't you know God gave you everything you need to be great?"

I have never forgotten those words from my grandmother. Those powerful words have cultivated me into the woman I am today. Despite my grandmother being my main caregiver, I also adopted my mother's perseverance and resilience. While my grandmother instilled a tenacity and willingness to overcome adversity in my life, my mother exemplified survival and hustle. I learned early that I was meant for bigger things that required my obedience. Both my grandmother and mother instilled fundamentals that contributed to the leader I am today. My life was blessed because of both of these women.

Leadership. Resilience. Self-Accountability.

This is the trajectory learned from both my mother and grandmother, which helped catapult my early childhood career. I found myself terminated from my job and I decided that no one should be in control of my destiny but God. I decided to stand on faith and move in his favor with boldness. By doing so, I created economic empowerment and wealth-building through a network of early childhood providers.

As a leader in early childhood education, I stand by the mantra of leadership that was instilled in me as a child. It is important that ECE professionals lead with integrity and respect for our colleagues and constituents in the field. The early childhood education field is comprised of 40 percent women of color. It is important that we use our voice and platform unapologetically. The children we serve deserve excellence and a confirmation of the greatness that they possess. It's amazing that within my tenure, I have been given the divine opportunity to encourage little brown girls, even as they experience some of the same emotions I did as a child.

There are four beautiful young girls in my program whom I lovingly call Princess Milla, Princess Jordan, Princess Zariah, and Princess Meghan. These four girls demonstrated similar feelings regarding their height. From the time these four entered my care, I poured into them empowerment and a confidence to embrace the gift of being tall.

"Stand tall. Express yourself. You are tall like me," I encouraged. These four young girls are phenomenal and flourishing in their authenticity.

It is my belief that the early childhood education professional must work to empower children, while empowering herself economically. I have been called to pour into others and provide a blazing blueprint to success and servant leadership. While serving young children and their families, we must encourage children to embrace their gifts and those qualities that make them unique and authentic.

We must affirm the gifts of each child and work to cultivate and nurture that child in order for the gifts to take flight. We must speak into children the wondrous possibilities that can lead to prosperous and fulfilling lives. In addition, we must create a standard of excellence in the lives of the children in our care that will remain with them into adulthood.

Leadership requires a willingness to move despite adversity and opposition.

AUTHENTIC

It requires that one walk in a determination that does not require the approval of naysayers. One must be completely focused on the goal ahead and proceed unapologetically in boldness.

With the life lessons and standards poured into me by my grandmother, I was determined to create my own seat at the table, create my own lane, and implement a ladder, in order to instill the same purpose into others. By learning to embrace my authenticity at a young age, I have developed a boldness that has assisted in creating my own "brand," I am a beautifully tall woman who is creating a legacy of leaders that will empower our future leaders!

My hope is that women begin to create their own seats at the table. Inclusion and diversity in early childhood education can be created by the individual. As leaders, we no longer have to wait on others to provide our opportunities. We can continue to lift as we climb, as we create empires that can change the trajectory of women in early childhood education.

It is our differences that can inspire and motivate others to lead. Through transparency and hard work, we can all achieve greatness while creating a revolution of dynamic future leaders.

JERLETHA MCDONALD

Jerletha McDonald is a social entrepreneur, family child care business consultant, national speaker, and visual podcast host. She owned and operated a family child care center, Nurturing Gifts Infant and Toddler Center for fifteen years. Jerletha is the founder and CEO of the ADFW Family Child Care Network. Jerletha is the host of her highly acclaimed Radio/Visual Podcast Show, "The Jerletha McDonald Show: Everything Childcare," where she discusses everything child care, and provides a platform for early childhood professionals to shine! Jerletha has fifteen years of experience in the field of early care childhood education. She has a special interest in economic security and leadership development of women and girls. In April of 2016, Jerletha was recognized by the Grand Prairie NAACP as one of the Most Influential Women in Business and has received numerous awards and recognition for business and child care excellence.

REFLECTION QUESTIONS

1 Jerletha's grandmother showed her a photograph of Naomi Campbell when she expressed her unhappiness with her height. What does representation mean to you? Did you have the opportunity to see images of people that looked like you during your childhood? In a society where white is the default, how can we offer a different experience in the places where we have power and influence?

2 Jerletha has found success through entrepreneurship, a common path for Black women in the United States. Why do you think that this career path is common in the Black community?

3 In the words of Jerletha's grandmother, "You must walk in your greatness. Don't you know God gave you everything you need to be great?" Consider the people and places that support you to walk in your greatness.

4 How can educators ensure that all of the children in their programs or communities have the opportunity to see themselves reflected in positive ways?

"I CARRY AND APPLY AN APPRECIATION AND UNDERSTANDING THAT ALL CHILDREN ARE FULL HUMAN BEINGS WITH THE CAPACITY TO RESPOND (IN VARYING DEGREES) TO INDIVIDUALIZED DEVELOPMENTALLY APPROPRIATE INTERACTIONS."

— CYNTHIA DAVIS-VANLOO

DEFINING
CYNTHIA DAVIS-VANLOO

I received an unexpected invitation to share my story for this anthology. Before beginning, I reflected on what having "a seat at the table" meant to me. I'd mostly heard the phrase used in reference to corporate structures and a desire for power and control, or leadership. It has never been in my nature to seek out positions of power or leadership, so the phrase wasn't one that I'd used in reference to my own experiences.

The immediate image that comes to mind when I think of "a seat at the table" is of a boardroom table. The group members gathered around the table are in business attire, and are predominantly white and predominantly male. They are making decisions that reflect the power and control they hold over others. The follow up image includes members that may be more racially and ethnically diverse and dressed more casually, who also make decisions that reflect the power and control they hold over others.

As a person who values community, collaboration, and collective decision making, I am resistant to having a seat at those types of tables. However, when I searched the meaning of seat at the table, I encountered this definition: "A position as a member of a group that makes decisions" (Macmillan, 2020). I used this definition to reimagine what a seat at the table can mean, and to guide the retrospective telling of my own story of finding my seat at the table.

My roots are in a large extended family of caregivers, educators, and creatives, who worked collectively to survive and thrive as well as possible under conditions of federally and socially sanctioned racial injustice, segregation, and forced integration. My mother was a nurse, despite her high school counselor advising her against it. She was told that since her mother was a domestic worker, she could only hope to be a domestic worker as well. She persisted in pursuing nursing school, all while being a young wife and mother, and encouraged her children to pursue any possibilities for their futures.

I was a caregiver in my family and community from a young age. As a four-year-old, I "defended" my older brother and sister from older kids who were teasing them. And as with many large extended families, I babysat many of my younger cousins until I moved away from them as an adult. This was my informal introduction to caring for children.

I entered the formal field of education shortly after graduating with a bachelor's degree in speech and hearing (speech pathology and audiology). I was fortunate to attend a small college that had a speech and language clinic on campus. Students could apply acquired knowledge and skills during their junior and senior undergraduate years. In larger colleges and universities at the time, this opportunity was often limited to graduate students. There I learned to make decisions about the treatment of clinic clients with faculty, clients, and peers. This early hands-on opportunity, along with college courses in sign language and close interactions with Black students from around the globe in our small Black Students Union (on a predominantly white campus in a predominantly white town) combined in beneficial ways I was not aware of at the time—I was learning collaborative decision making and community building outside of my home community.

By the time I finished college, I knew that I did not have passion for pursuing speech pathology or audiology as a career. But I did have passion for caring for children and witnessing the evolution of their growth and development. A friend worked at a residential school for children with multiple disabilities, where there was an opening for an assistant teacher position. Although I didn't feel qualified as a classroom teacher, I was attracted to the idea of working with children with disabilities. As it turned out, the assistant teacher position encompassed much more than classroom teaching. My personal, academic, and practical experience aligned well with the job duties. I applied for and got the position.

The residential school schedule included classroom time in the morning, lunch break, and more classroom time until 3 p.m. This was followed by "activities of daily living" until dinner time. After dinner was recreational/free time followed by bedtime routines. The children had various combinations of moderate-to-severe physical, developmental, sensory, and cognitive disabilities. As an assistant teacher, I was often with children from their afternoon classroom time through bedtime, so I got to know the children individually. I connected with those children that had the capacity to connect with others, and cared for all of them.

There was a certified special education teacher for each classroom. That teacher created lesson plans and IEPs (Individualized Education Programs) and was with children during the "school" hours. The special education teachers I worked with sought input from the assistant teachers, who worked closely with the students, when making decisions around lesson planning and IEPs. This appeared to indicate that I had "a seat at the table." However, I realized that I had different expectations for what some of the students were capable of than was written into their IEPs and lesson plans. So, although I appeared to have a seat at the table, I had no power to make decisions at that table.

> "... ALTHOUGH I APPEARED TO HAVE A SEAT AT THE TABLE, I HAD NO POWER TO MAKE DECISIONS AT THAT TABLE."
>
> — CYNTHIA DAVIS-VANLOO

I did have the power to act on my own knowledge and experience with the students in everyday interactions with them, as I worked toward achieving IEP goals and lesson plans. For children who were non-verbal and had the cognitive and manual capacity, I introduced and reinforced new sign language vocabulary (I had more American Sign Language skills than most staff and faculty at that time). For children who were verbal, had functional levels of cognitive capacities and had some physical capacity, I would teach and encourage self-help skills beyond what may have been in their IEPs.

There were two girls I worked with who had different types of severe cerebral palsy, "a group of disorders that affect a person's ability to move and maintain balance and posture" (Center for Disease Control and Prevention, 2019). Both girls were early adolescents, non-verbal, and had some control over their head and eye movements. I learned that they had not had opportunities to play with materials that were not considered directly educational or therapeutic. I purchased sets of paper dolls and played paper dolls with them. One of the girls used eye direction to show me what outfits and actions she wanted her dolls to make. The other girl had limited control of one arm and hand and could physically indicate which outfits she wanted on her dolls. I would then make up scenarios that would change based on the girls' reactions and non-verbal cues. Their reactions (laughter and excitement) let me know that they enjoyed and benefited from this type of engagement, so I offered them that and similar activities regularly.

There are many more stories that I cherish from that work experience that occurred more than thirty-five years ago. I loved working with the young people at that residential school. I enjoyed getting to know each of them and learning what they were capable of, not just what was "disabled" or "broken" in them. At that time, I didn't know about social and emotional development. It wasn't something that was identified in the IEPs and lesson plans, and it wasn't a part of my undergraduate education. I look back on the experience from my current understanding of social and emotional development, and realize I was attempting to support each student's social and emotional development, along with their identified physical and cognitive developmental goals.

I learned a lot working with children with severe or multiple disabilities. I carry and apply an appreciation and understanding that all children are full human beings with the capacity to respond (in varying degrees) to individualized developmentally appropriate interactions. I also learned that not everyone perceived the children the same way I did, especially at the institution's administrative level. The year I resigned from the assistant teacher position, the administrators made decisions about classroom changes and groupings that didn't seem to take into account the children's needs and relationships, or the special education teachers' recommendations. As an assistant teacher, I definitely did not have a seat at the decision-making table. The students that I'd been working with for almost four years were separated and placed in different classrooms with different teachers. It felt like a type of "violence" that I didn't want to participate in. But, I left believing I made a positive difference in the lives of each student I engaged with while I was there.

When I left the assistant teaching job, I moved across the United States from the Northeast to the Pacific Northwest. Soon afterward, a family member introduced me to a child care center that was hiring. Gentle Dragon Childcare Center operated as a collective, in which staff collaboratively shared the responsibilities of running the center. Though people had titles such as director, administrator, cook, teacher, and assistant, the duties under each title were shared–no individual had sole responsibility for a role, or power over anyone else. Additionally, the center was rooted in an anti-bias and social justice framework that was unique in the 1980s. Staff and families represented racial, ethnic, linguistic, refugee and immigrant, LGBT (the acronym used at that time), ability, and socio-economic diversity. It was a small community where I truly had a seat at the table.

DEFINING

I was at Gentle Dragon for two years before leaving to attend school full-time for American Sign Language interpreter training. My experience at Gentle Dragon permanently impacted my understanding of what an equitable, anti-biased "table" could look and feel like. I hold that as a valued experience that continues to shape my perspectives and choices about professional communities, rooms, and tables I participate in.

During and after completing the interpreter training program, I was involved in the local Deaf community in a variety of capacities. In addition to developing friendships, my other community involvement included working as an ASL interpreter, domestic violence advocate, and TDD (telecommunications device for the deaf) relay operator. Building on this experience, I moved back across the country to pursue a master's degree in deafness rehabilitation. It was a funded accelerated program that had an equity and social justice perspective toward serving people with hearing impairments, and deaf communities.

After completing my master's degree, I was hired as a social worker doing casework, counseling, and parent education with racially and ethnically diverse families. The parents or children in these families were deaf (physical disability) and/or Deaf (cultural and linguistic identity), and the children were at risk of abuse or neglect due to being underserved, under-resourced, or because of limited parenting skills. This job presented a variety of opportunities to engage in creative problem solving to support families. Although it was challenging, there were many aspects of the job that I enjoyed, especially as clients gained confidence and competence in their own possibilities. I developed invaluable skills, knowledge, and understandings. I also felt that this was a collaborative work environment where I had a seat at the table. The supervisor maintained a culture of collective work and responsibility that aligned with mine.

Like many work experiences, there were aspects of the job that I didn't get any pleasure in doing and didn't feel that I did particularly well. So, after taking a medical leave to manage a difficult pregnancy and premature childbirth, I decided not to return to the job. Instead, I did freelance interpreting and parented until I moved with my family to the Pacific Northwest—again for me, while it was the first time for my husband and son—landing in the same city where I'd lived before.

During the years that I'd lived elsewhere, the preschool I previously worked at had closed and the people I'd worked with had moved on, though most were still in the geographical area. I resumed personal relationships with some, and made new connections as well, forming a multiracial, multiethnic, and multicultural equity and social justice-centered community. Through those community connections, I re-entered the field of early childhood care and education, first as a substitute preschool teacher and ECE teacher trainer, then in child care licensing and regulation.

Substitute teaching reminded me of my love for working directly with young children, witnessing and supporting the possibilities for their development. I regularly substituted at a small center that allowed me freedom to develop lesson plans and activities in the classrooms. I enjoyed developing relationships with the children and their families, as well as creating or scaffolding interest-based activities. The center directors created a collaborative culture that invited me to have a seat at the table, even though I was a substitute. I felt welcomed and valued at that "table."

While I was substitute teaching, freelance ASL interpreting, and facilitating ECE trainings and workshops, one of my community connections told me about a full-time job opening where she worked in child care licensing. We discussed the job description and the culture of the office. It seemed like an opportunity to use and build upon my knowledge, skills, and experience. I applied and was subsequently hired as a family home child care licensor. I enjoyed the work, my colleagues, and the office culture. It felt like a small collaborative community that largely embraced culturally relevant/anti-bias practices. It also felt like a familiar culture, because I knew two of my licensing colleagues from my earlier time working at Gentle Dragon Childcare Center.

Our licensing unit was a small division within a large administration in a larger government human services agency. I worked with FCC providers in some of the top one hundred most diverse zip codes in the United States, at that time. In this environment, I felt like I had a seat at the table, and I participated in decision-making about the work I did.

Four years into my experience as a FCC licensor, the supervisor for our unit announced his retirement. He invited me to apply for the supervisor position and described why he believed I was qualified. Most of my co-workers in the unit encouraged me to apply for the position, so they would continue to have a supervisor who knew the work we had been doing, the communities we worked with, and the culture of the diverse unit. I wasn't seeking a leadership position, but I was willing to apply for the position to support my co-workers, who I saw as passionate and dedicated to ensuring children had equitable early learning opportunities that met minimum requirements. I applied for and was hired into the position of licensing supervisor.

Transitioning from being a licensor to the licensing supervisor position had many challenges. In addition to developing the skill sets needed for the new role, the relationships I had with my former peers shifted as I moved into being their supervisor. I grieved the loss of those relationships as they had been, as I tried to sustain an internal culture where everyone had a seat at the table, even if I held the responsibility for the decisions made.

With the continued evolution of the child care licensing agency into a multitiered hierarchy of "tables" I became increasingly aware of how the expectations of the organization did not match my identity. I entered licensing because I believed that no child deserved less than the minimum health and safety requirements in licensed child care. I also believed it was important to develop relationships with people in order to work effectively with culturally and linguistically diverse communities toward meeting and maintaining those minimum requirements, and encourage best practices. I started off in a unit and at a "table" where that was valued. That changed with the organization's growth, evolution, and emphasis on timelines and "accountability" over the reality of working with diverse communities. I accepted the supervisor position because I thought I, a Black African American woman, could support my culturally and linguistically diverse staff to do their best work under the scrutiny of systemic racism and microaggressions.

DEFINING

During a professional development event, the presenter, Dr. Debra R. Sullivan, asked the room of employees, "If you can't operate with authenticity and integrity, why are you here? Why are you doing this job?" I reflected on this question as I continued in the supervisor position for another year or so. I continued until it became clear that I had limited real power to act with authenticity and integrity, and ethically. I was a supervisor who believed no child in licensed care deserved less than the minimum health and safety requirements, and that collaborative relationships with my capable and competent staff and their relationships with their child care providers were important in the work. There was no real "seat at the table" for me. I felt silenced and devalued in many ways. My attempts to find a seat at this new table took a toll on my physical, mental, and emotional health. I ended up choosing to leave this job with thirty days' notice and no other job prospect, believing that my staff deserved to have someone other than me in the position who understood and aligned with the new organizational culture and priorities supporting their work.

After leaving the licensing agency, I collaborated with a friend to create a consulting business focused on anti-racism, social justice, and equity in education. Although I didn't prioritize my business, I learned from this experience that it was possible to visualize and build my own table and invite others to that table. I also began community volunteering that I didn't have the time or energy to participate in when I was in child care licensing. I was invited to join a task force that advocated for culturally relevant, equitable, early learning opportunities for Black children. And I was invited to join the board of trustees for a non-profit organization that provided culturally relevant/anti-bias training and workshops for early learning professionals that served Black children and children of color. The members of the task force were all African American women who were passionate about working toward equitable culturally relevant opportunities for Black children. The non-profit had equally passionate Black folks and allies who valued community and collaboration. They welcomed me to their "tables" and embraced what I brought to the table. These were deeply healing experiences.

One of the task force members was a coordinator for the ECE program at a local community college. She invited me to apply to teach a sign language class for adults working with young children. I submitted my application and was hired as adjunct (part-time) faculty. The coordinator saw value in my varied ECE experiences and invited me to teach other classes for the program. Although I didn't have any significant decision-making power in the program, there was a culture of collaboration and professional freedom that I appreciated and benefited from, as a person and as an educator. The culture of collaboration and professional freedom within the program is one of the reasons I continue to serve as adjunct faculty at that institution.

In addition to higher education teaching, I also contracted to facilitate professional development trainings/workshops and quality improvement consulting in early learning. I didn't have any real decision-making power

> "I LEARNED FROM THIS EXPERIENCE THAT IT WAS POSSIBLE TO VISUALIZE AND BUILD MY OWN TABLE AND INVITE OTHERS TO THAT TABLE."
>
> — CYNTHIA DAVIS-VANLOO

at these various "tables." However, each situation provided opportunities for me to build relationships, community, and collaboration. I could provide information and reflective practices to help decision makers move toward equitable developmentally appropriate practices in early learning.

I enjoyed the contract work and found joy and inspiration in teacher education and professional development. It was work that I felt aligned well with my beliefs and values, and I felt passionate about it. But it wasn't consistent work. I thought that at some point I would have to find full-time work in an organization or agency for my own financial stability and predictability. Before I pursued that, I wanted to learn how I might better understand the cultures and power dynamics of predominantly white organizational structures. I wanted to develop the knowledge and skills that would allow me to work effectively in an organization from a position of authenticity and integrity. I wanted to explore how education systems and structures work, and how they might function more equitably. I chose to do that by pursuing a doctoral degree in education.

My doctoral journey was one of those, "be careful what you ask for, you just might get it" experiences. The college's tagline was "Education for change," and my concentration was in curriculum, teaching, learning, and leadership. I experienced a lot of growth (and accompanying growing pains) as I developed and expanded my knowledge, language, and understandings of complex structural and systemic oppression in my concentration areas and beyond. I also developed (and continue to develop) greater critical analysis skills that allow me to recognize ways in which we are socialized to participate in and perpetuate oppression as normal. The journey was difficult and transformative on many levels. I learned to better value, trust and use my voice to share my perspectives and understandings. And, it resulted in me developing a critical social justice, anti-racist and equity lens that will continue to evolve.

This reflection on my experiences with, and what it means to have "a seat at the table" is timely. After finishing my doctoral degree, I'm in a transitional period figuring out how I will apply and share my learning in alignment with who I have grown into and continue to grow into. As I reflect on my past experiences and future possibilities, I'm asking these questions:

- What types of "tables" will I seek out, accept invitations to, or build?
- Who does a "table" benefit, and who does it harm or hinder?
- How necessary is it for me to be at a "table?"

To answer these questions, I first need to reimagine the concept of the "table." This retrospective has provided an opportunity to do that considering the Macmillan (2020) definition of "a position as a member of a group that makes decisions." My responses to these questions will be based on my perspectives in the moment. They will undoubtedly evolve and change as my knowledge and understandings continue to evolve and change.

This writing has been a self-reflective exercise on what the phrase, "a seat at the table" has meant, currently means, and may mean in the future to me as a

DEFINING

Black African American woman in the fields of education and early childhood. I complete this writing with some realizations and a broader understanding of the concept of "a seat at the table" in relation to my own experiences. I realize that I have had seats at many "tables" that fed my passion and aligned with my core values of community, collaboration, integrity, and authenticity along my journey in ECE that did not fit my image of "the boardroom." I understand that I was invited to each of those "tables" by someone I was in collaboration or community with. I also realize that when I have operated with authenticity and integrity, others have recognized and valued my potential contributions at a table where they held membership, and invited me to join them. In turn, I can invite others to join me at a "table," or replace me when it is time for me to leave.

Additionally, I can redefine "a position as a member of a group that makes decisions" (Macmillan, 2020) as "a position as a member of a community that makes decisions." In community we can construct, deconstruct and rebuild tables, share tables or use tables to stand on as platforms as we choose in order to impact change toward anti-racism and equity in ECE. If I use my voice with authenticity and integrity, act in alignment with my values in community and collaboration, and support others in doing the same, change happens. I believe we all have the capacity to make decisions that impact others whenever we are in shared space. I look forward to the possibilities I will encounter as I continue to explore what it can mean to define "a seat at the table" as "a position as a member of a community that makes decisions."

CYNTHIA DAVIS-VANLOO

Cynthia Davis-Vanloo has over thirty-five years of experience in early childhood education and related fields including working with children and adults with disabilities in classroom and residential settings, early childhood education and center management, casework and counseling with children and families, parent education, American Sign Language interpreting, child care regulation, and ECE training and coaching. She has served as part-time faculty in the Early Childhood Education Department at North Seattle College for over ten years.

Cynthia holds a doctoral degree in education with a concentration in curriculum, teaching, learning, and leadership.

REFLECTION QUESTIONS

1 Cynthia defines the phrase "finding a seat at the table" for us and uses the definition to reflect on her own "seats at the table" and to create a new definition for herself. Why is the concept of finding a seat at the table something we even need to discuss? How have Black women been excluded from groups with power in the past?

2 Cynthia found herself in a leadership position for the licensing agency where she worked mostly because she felt a responsibility to her co-workers. This position created suffering for her and she sacrificed her own mental and physical health until she made the decision to leave. Have you ever stuck with something because you felt a sense of responsibility even though it was hurting you? How might Black women carry the responsibility of others in ways that are different from other groups of women?

3 Much of Cynthia's professional success came from her connection with others who noticed her work. What sorts of connections do you have that might help you to find your seat at the table? What connections might you pursue? If you already have a seat at the table, how might you make room for new voices?

4 Cynthia redefines a seat at the table to mean a community of people making decisions, rather than a small/elite group. Do you have experience being part of a group or community that makes decisions together?

"THE WAY OTHER PEOPLE SEE ME DOESN'T MAKE ME OR BREAK ME. I WILL CONTINUE TO BE WHO I AM AND WHAT I AM."

— JOYCE JACKSON

DETERMINED
JOYCE JACKSON

I'm just a Black girl who loves working with children. I've known since the age of five that I wanted to be a teacher. I love being a part of how children grow and learn, and I get joy from knowing that what I do now will be a huge part of what our country will be in the future.

I've been working in the ECE field for over thirty years, and I've been at my current program for the past ten. This is the first time that I've worked in a school outside of my own community. When I first started there, believe me, I thought I had made a huge mistake. The only thing that made me stay there was my determination to not be run off by privileged, rich, white people.

I was used to being with people who were just like me. I worked with young single moms and dads whose skin color was just like mine. They had similar stories to mine, and we could relate to each other on a cultural level. It's hard being the only Black teacher in a school with one Black kid and, I believe, one Asian child. Both were adopted by white families and brought here from their native country. They were also both in my classroom.

In the classroom that first year of the center's opening, I was not seen as a teacher by parents or by my own co-workers. I would cry a lot in my car on my breaks and didn't want to return to that school after the first three or four days. I had parents only talk directly to their child, even though they heard me say good morning. This ignoring would happen at pick up, too. It was like I was invisible to them. I kept going back and letting them know I was there and I'd be there for the long haul. They had the problems, not me. I've had white coworkers tell me that my opinions were not valued as much as those of my white coworkers. I didn't believe this until I saw it happen with my own eyes. One day, I brought up a situation that was going on with my co-teacher. She was regularly late to work and it was starting to become a problem. I discussed it with my boss because she asked how we were doing as a team. She let me know that she'd take care of it that day. Well, the next day came and the situation happened again, and I asked my co-teacher if our boss talked to her about this. She said no. I was so mad and upset, but I just let it continue for the rest of the school year.

The next year, we worked together again and things were the same. Then another teacher, who happened to be white, saw my co-teacher arriving late one morning when she was supposed to already be at work, and reported her to our boss. My boss pulled her into the office that day for a conversation, and then got mad at me for not saying anything to her about my co-teacher's chronic lateness. When I told her why, she apologized repeatedly and said that she valued me, and was so sorry for making me feel like I didn't matter. She acknowledged that she really felt bad, knowing now that she ever made me feel that way.

DETERMINED

One year, we got a new student a couple months after the first day of school. Let's call her Jayda. Jayda came in bright and bubbly. She was a friendly little Black girl ready to make friends. A week or so into Jayda's new journey at our school, my teaching team noticed that she needed some help joining playgroups and making new friends.

One morning, we teachers decided to pair up the kids instead of letting them choose their own partners. We chose for Jayda to go with a friend we'll call Cassie, who we had also noticed needed some support engaging in play. We made the choice to put these two girls together as partners.

Jayda was excited and ran over to Cassie, who was white, and put her hand out. Cassie drew her hand back quickly. We asked what was the problem and Cassie said, "I don't want to hold her hand, it's brown!"

Jayda got upset and cried and Cassie just stood there with her hands pulled behind her. I ran to hug Jayda and let her know that I'd be her partner, and we removed Cassie for a short discussion away from the other kids. We then put both girls together with all three teachers and talked about what happened. We explained to Cassie about hurting others' feelings and saying things that aren't kind. By this time, I was feeling just like Jayda, hurt and sad, and wondering why Cassie would say something like that. Where did she get that from? What was she being taught?

I purposely chose to put both girls at my lunch table a few days later, and when it was Cassie's turn to pass food to Jayda, she refused to do it. I got out of my chair and went to Cassie and began to speak softly to her. I asked her to pass the food, but instead she quickly pulled away from me. She didn't want me to touch her or be physically close to her. By this point, I was done! I stepped back and asked the other teachers, "Did you see this?" They all nodded. I needed a moment.

I immediately had a conversation with my boss about this child, how she made me feel, and how much it hurt me, because that child didn't even know me. She didn't want to get to know me and already had some thoughts in her head about the color of my skin being a bad thing. I was mad for Jayda and now for myself, because obviously Cassie had some false information coming from Lord knows where about people who don't have the same color skin as hers. Seeing this kind of blind prejudice coming from a child was an entirely new experience for me. What were we going to do about this?

It's hard being treated differently or even ignored because of the color of your skin by an adult, but when this behavior comes from a child, it hits you in a whole different way. Why? Because this is a learned behavior, so it was obvious to me that this child had never been around Black or brown people, and also that this child had the idea that Black- and brown-skinned people were not "good," and were not people that she wanted to be around.

> "SEEING THIS KIND OF BLIND PREJUDICE COMING FROM A CHILD WAS AN ENTIRELY NEW EXPERIENCE FOR ME. WHAT WERE WE GOING TO DO ABOUT THIS?"
>
> — JOYCE JACKSON

"I WILL CONTINUE TO SHOW AND TEACH THESE KIDS ABOUT FAIRNESS AND EQUITY AND EQUALITY IN A WAY THAT THEY UNDERSTAND IT, AND PUSH THEIR PARENTS TO CARRY ON THESE SAME TALKS WITH THEIR KIDS AT HOME."

— JOYCE JACKSON

This is when I decided that she and I were going to be BEST FRIENDS. I started a small group of friends with her and four other kids in the room that were having challenges around sharing and being kind to others. They named themselves The Friends Group. Each week, I'd take them out of the room to a smaller shared space and we'd have talks about fairness and being nice and what it means to be a friend. We always talked about loving ourselves and the color of our skin. I would bring up ways that we were different, but also invited them to say which ways we were the same. We read books about feelings and how not to hurt our friends and family with our words and actions. We talked about how hurtful words made us feel. Whenever Cassie and I were alone, I would ask her why she didn't want to be my friend or hold my hand. She'd always reply, "I just don't want to."

My teaching team and I decided to host a meeting with the parents to talk about the things we were observing with this group of children. My co-teachers and I had questions about exposing white kids to people of color, and about choosing the right language to use with children about people who are different from you. I was surprised that more than one of our families admitted to never having had a person of color in their home or as a close friend. We didn't get far with this group of parents about the kids not wanting to be friends with other kids because of skin color, but what we did get from the parents was a bunch of questions about what they could do about this problem. They wondered how they could talk to their kids about accepting people's differences and being friends with all kinds of people. I was so frustrated after this meeting, especially when we talked about preparing kids for kindergarten and grade school. What I have to prepare my kids for is totally different than what white people have to prepare their kids for. They just didn't get it!

There was a time when we had a permanent substitute teacher for all rooms; an older Black woman. She didn't look anything like me, and she worked with me in my room a lot in the summer. Regardless, one parent kept calling me by the other woman's name.

The first couple of times, I nicely corrected her. Then she did it again, this time in front of her kid. The child yelled, "That's Joyce, stop calling her Theresa. She keeps telling you her name." That parent apologized to me twice the next day.

People like this and situations like this are the reason why I do what I do every day. I will continue to show and teach these kids about fairness and equity and equality in a way that they understand it, and push their parents to carry on these same talks with their kids at home.

The way other people see me doesn't make me or break me. I will continue to be who I am and what I am. Because at the end of the day, they are the ones with the problem, not me.

JOYCE JACKSON

Joyce Jackson has been an early childhood educator for over thirty years. She is a wife, mother of three and grandmother of twelve. During the first twenty years of her career, Joyce worked in two programs that served low income families in her community. In 2011, Joyce joined the staff of Epiphany Early Learning Center where she is currently working in the pre-K classroom. Joyce is proud to share that she was the first teacher of color hired at her center and she is just as passionate about her job now as she was thirty years ago!

REFLECTION QUESTIONS

1 When Joyce noticed that her boss was addressing her white co-workers' concerns and not hers, she decided to stop speaking up. Have you ever felt silenced by someone in power? How might you provide space for all voices to feel heard?

2 Joyce shares a painful story about a little girl with some racist comments and actions that hurt her deeply. How can educators prepare themselves to address these sorts of situations when they happen in their classrooms? What role do white educators have in supporting their Black colleagues when faced with racism?

3 You can see through her story that Joyce has a strong sense of self. Where do you think she draws this strength from? What are some ways that educators can support Black children in their communities to cultivate a strong self-image?

"I AM NOT A 'KICK-DOWN-THE-DOOR' KIND OF PERSON. BUT I DO HAVE A STRONG SENSE OF JUSTICE, I AM WILLING TO SPEAK UP FOR MYSELF AND OTHERS AND TO TAKE EMOTIONAL RISKS."

— NADIYAH TAYLOR

LIMITLESS
NADIYAH TAYLOR

My name is Nadiyah Alicia Faquir Taylor. I am a full-time professor at Las Positas Community College, the chair of the early care and education program, and a coach/trainer on anti-bias education. I am a former preschool teacher, a wife, and mother of two mixed-race children. I had the honor of contributing to "Anti-Bias Education for Young Children and Ourselves" and "From Teaching to Thinking: A Pedagogy for Reimagining Our Work." When I consider the question, "How did I get here," what comes to mind are strong female role models, critical experiences of marginalization, family support for education, and my willingness to be vulnerable in public. I am not a "kick-down-the-door" kind of person. But I do have a strong sense of justice, I am willing to speak up for myself and others and to take emotional risks. These qualities, combined with my great luck in meeting leaders in the field, have created situations where I was asked to "come to the table."

I have been fascinated by children all my life and wanted to be a teacher for as long as I can remember. Whatever the role, my work for the past 27 years has had one focus, for education to be equitable for all children and to support teachers to make that happen. I am from a family of strong women and have followed a career path governed by women. I am so blessed to have met many wonderful women along my journey. The women often held power in their fields, and they often saw qualities in me that I did not see in myself; urging me to go higher and make room for myself and my unique voice. At the same time, due to systemic racism in education, both environmentally and in leadership, I have either put, or found, myself in racially uncomfortable work environments, classrooms, and schools repeatedly in my life. With resilience, persistence, openness, and self-reflection, I have taken all that I can from each environment to continue to move my agenda forward.

I am a product of the 1970s post-civil rights movement. I grew up in Chicago seeing posters in my community with the slogan "Black is Beautiful" and reading my grandparents' Ebony and Jet magazines, which showcased Black America in positive and interesting ways. My life in Chicago was one of being cocooned within extended family—aunts, cousins, uncles, and almost weekly visits with both sets of grandparents—along with my four siblings and my parents. I spent lots of time with my maternal and paternal grandparents, all of whom worked outside of the home in their own businesses. My maternal grandmother, Katherine Simpkins, owned a beauty salon and worked until she was seventy-five. I spent many hours there, watching "the stories" (soap operas) with my grandmother, and learning about the adult world of Black people in Chicago by listening to the conversations between my grandmother and her clients. My paternal grandparents, Charles and Virginia Charlton, owned a butcher shop and a small convenience store during their lifetime together. While I don't remember spending time in the businesses of my paternal grandparents, the stories of their work were part of the fabric of my childhood; I learned about the neighborhood and the people within it. My paternal grandfather had also been a Pullman porter, and while I did not understand the full significance of that until I was older, I knew from a young age that it was a point of pride for him.

As best as I can remember, I did not know any woman who did not work outside of the home. In addition to my grandmothers, my aunts also worked, as travel agents, advertising executives, and police officers. This was true not only of my family members but of all Black women in my life and my neighborhoods. It was explicitly taught and modeled that Black women worked, that's just what you did. It was a natural part of my vision for adulthood that I, too, would work and if I had a family, would also be present for them. All the adults in my family were partnered, and their partners/husbands worked too. I am so grateful for these wonderful examples in my life. All the men in my family were consistently supportive of me, they expected me to be successful and did not think that women should be held back from exerting their talent.

Despite strong male role models, when I think about my professional journey, I think about the examples set by women: their nurturing and sometimes not so gentle "nudges" to live up to my promise as a Black woman, to believe I can and should be more. My mother set a strong example as a young mother who went to college and earned a master's degree while working and raising five children. She was committed to her children and was, at least to my child's eye, tireless. She worked several part-time jobs when I was young, scheduling them so that she could be there when my brother and I got home from school. I didn't realize until I was an older child that she would often work late into the night, researching topics for graduate students and writing magazine pieces. Yet she was up before all of us, making breakfast, combing hair, getting lunches together and sending us off to school. She eventually began working full-time when I was a young teenager. Our whole family worked as a team to support the family's success during this transition. Getting your education and working hard to make the family function successfully were important lessons that shaped me. My family's love of education and intellectual curiosity was a huge asset in my educational journey.

It is also clear to me that racism, sexism, classism, and heteronormative socialization were, and are, key elements of my journey. I cannot separate my early understanding that women worked, and worked hard, from the fact that I am Black, that my early years were often very economically challenging, and that I was born shortly after the height of both the civil rights and women's rights movements. I was taught that Black women worked because we had to; we did not have the luxury of being parents full-time. We had to work and still be the "woman of the house." I was told that Black women worked hard not only because we cared for our families, but because we are held to different and unfair standards. We are paid less for the work we do, because we are both women and Black. Our voices, knowledge, and life experiences are discounted for the same reasons. We must be careful to not be "too Black" but to also be the voice of the "Black perspective."

I heard countless stories of racist interactions with clients, bosses, and co-workers: city workers, police, social workers, and schools. Some in my family gave me the lesson of quiet stoicism in the face of constant racism. My parents were seen by some as "Black radicals," which I think they were quite fine with. My siblings and I were taught Black history at home, discussed the racism inherent in our everyday experiences, and when we watched TV together my parents routinely pointed out racism, sexism, and classism in the shows.

We converted to Islam when I was very young, both for religious and political reasons. At that time in Chicago, Islam was both a positive spiritual practice and a focal point for community activism, which appealed to my parents. Islam was a salient part of my home culture and continues to influence my understanding and experience with being part of multiple marginalized communities. Paying attention to the world around you and examining systems of power were other key messages from my parents.

I also grew up knowing that Black leaders were killed at a high rate during and after the heart of the Civil Rights movement. This violence was sometimes state sanctioned and at other times vigilante-driven. I learned early that I was not to go into certain parts of Chicago, because Black people were not welcomed there and would be harmed. The connection between violence and racism was clear to me from a young age and it stays with me now, as I raise my own children. My mother recently put these feelings so succinctly when she wrote, "I had an expectation of [violence], sitting on the back burner of my awareness. Don't imagine constant anxiety, or anything like that. See instead the awareness you have of your heart beating but pay no real attention to it until it beats too fast—or stops beating!" The consistent background awareness of racism shapes me and my teaching and all my professional interactions.

By nature, I am a meditator; I see multiple ways to solve a problem, I want everyone to be happy, and I don't like conflict. At the same time, I have a strong sense of justice and identify with the underdog. I cry easily and as a child, I wore my feelings openly. Being raised in the 70s, I was caught between generational messages about how to be a girl and how to be Black. You can't let people take advantage of you. Be strong. Be nice, don't swear, be good. Take care of yourself, don't depend on a man to make you whole, but look for a good man to marry. Straighten your hair to look professional; don't straighten your hair to show that you are proud of your heritage. Be a "good" girl who follows the rules, crosses her legs and wears a purse. Be a "bad" girl, who is a tomboy, earns her own money, and questions authority. It was quite confusing to know how to incorporate all these disparate messages into who I was becoming. It is important to say here that as a child, I passionately resisted my parents and family telling me that racism was alive and well. I did not want that to be true. Learning that hard truth over my lifetime has left me with deep wounds and a cynicism that is sometimes hard to battle. But, my friend, Louise Derman-Sparks, reminds me that, "Without hope there can be no change," and that "everyone can change, some people just die before they do."

Racism and classism impacted my education in distinct ways. In all of my school experiences, as a Black girl/woman I have either been in the numerical minority of the school or, because of tracking, a numerical minority in my advanced classes. This has profoundly shaped my feelings about education and the experience of minoritized communities within it. I had a pretty great and diverse elementary school education because my parents fought for me to be bused to a magnet school on the other side of the city; the schools where we lived weren't as good. Busing to integrate the schools was happening at that time and I was a beneficiary. I learned to speak French in elementary school, got to have music and art classes regularly and was in a gifted reading program that collaborated with the Art Institute of Chicago. However, like many things, this well-rounded education came with costs. I lived far away from friends, my home life was mostly unlike the home lives of many at the school, and my Black friends in the neighborhood slowly distanced themselves from me because I was now "too white." The curriculum did not reflect my life or the lives of those around me. My high school was primarily middle/upper middle class and about 85 percent Black. Due to tracking, though, I was often one of a few people of color in my classes, leaving me again ostracized from my larger community of Black classmates. My family was not middle-class at this time, so there were significant disconnects here, too. I graduated near the top of my high school class and was accepted by many colleges. This achievement was soured when two of my best friends, both white, told me I got into those colleges only because I was Black. Microaggressions like these have influenced my sense of self and feelings about my competence. I hate to use a cliché, but I have certainly experienced imposter syndrome as a Black woman throughout my professional life.

I earned a bachelor's degree in psychology and a master's in human development; the master's allows me to teach in California community colleges. Both my undergraduate and graduate experiences were in places where I was a numerical minority on campus in all of my classes, and often among the lower income students there. I was trying to find my identity as a Black woman in all these spaces where I never quite felt that I fit in. These intersections of race-gender-social class have been drivers of my professional passion for teaching young children and working hard to make a better, more just future for them. I want them to experience an education where they are seen, their experiences and languages are validated, and where all children are taught to see unfairness and work to change it.

Making room at the table? I try to be transparent and honest; I am vulnerable when needed, and I try not to be hurtful. I am compassionate by nature, and this allows to me find the humanity in many situations. I think that helps me make connections and relationships of trust with people, even as we tackle difficult conversations.

I believe in the healing nature of gratitude. I value all my ancestors who came before, and I believe they want me to live whole, happy, and with my head held high. They fought and died for me to have this right. Despite imposter syndrome, multiple systems of oppression, and my own internal bent toward niceness, my journey has taught me that we take the hardships of life, smooth them out, and then lay the path for the next generation.

LIMITLESS

I must end by saying thank you. Thank you...

- first and always to my mother! You see each of your children through a lens of love, always providing needed guidance and life experience;
- to my sisters, and all the women in my extended family—you are models of love, strength, resilience, and revolutionary spirit;
- to my brothers, father, and all the male members of my family for embodying love, joy, service, and sacrifice;
- to my husband and life partner, who pushes me, cares for me, and helps me to move always closer to my dreams;
- to my children who push me to be courageous every day;
- to the many women friends and colleagues who saw in me something special that should be nurtured, and then provided me the scaffolding needed to reach higher goals; and
- to the writers and thought leaders who helped frame my understanding of the role of education in society and how it should be implemented, including a very special thank you to Louise Derman-Sparks, whose work has been a consistent light through many tunnels.

We all need mentors and guides in our lives. Those of us from marginalized identities also need to be explicitly and authentically told, "You can do this," and then given the opportunities and skills to fly!

NADIYAH TAYLOR

Nadiyah Taylor has been working in the field of ECE since 1990. She has taught all ages of children from infants up through eleven-year-olds. Nadiyah has done parent workshops and parent-child classes. For the last fifteen years, she has worked as a diversity/equity consultant to schools, conducting workshops on anti-bias education and family relationships. She has been a college instructor for fifteen years and has been at Las Positas College since 2009, where she is chair of the ECE department.

REFLECTION QUESTIONS

1 Nadiyah shared the sometimes conflicting messages she received as a child about how to be a Black woman. What messages did you receive about who you were supposed to be? How did you internalize those messages?

2 At the end of her story, Nadiyah called out the women, many white, who helped her to find her voice and her way. What role do white women play in supporting equity in work and school environments?

3 What has mentorship meant to you in your career progression?

4 Nadiyah talks about her experience feeling "imposter syndrome" (a phenomenon prevalent to high achievers where someone finds difficulty internalizing and accepting their own success, often attributing it to luck). Recall a time that you have felt like you weren't good enough or didn't belong in a space. Why do you think that women are more likely to experience this feeling?

"SOMETIMES IT IS NOT ABOUT FINDING YOUR SPACE AT THE TABLE, BUT BUILDING YOUR OWN TABLE WITH LIKE-MINDED INDIVIDUALS."

— BRANDY D. JAMES

REASSURANCE
BRANDY D. JAMES

From the art table to the conference table.

I remember the smell of crayons and construction paper the first day of Head Start. It was a warm summer day. I was dressed in my new shoes and pink romper. I was so excited to be picked up on the school bus in front of my grandparents' house in a small, rural town. I knew I was going to have a wonderful first day of preschool.

I gathered my small bag off of the school bus, walked down the stairs and into the school building to see my aunt Jill, one of the teachers in the school. We were lined up at the entrance and led down a hallway to our classroom. I remember sitting next to a little boy who raised his hand and asked if he could change seats because he was not allowed to sit by me. I did not know why, but my classroom teacher moved him to another seat.

I should have started the story with some background information. I was a little Black girl. I had huge pink-framed glasses that magnified the entire world for me to see. I was also partially blind. I lived with my grandparents in a town of about 2,500 people, and all of the children who looked like me were my close and distant family members.

I knew I was going to have a wonderful first day of preschool.

As the half day progressed, I was met with some looks, grins, and remarks about my looks, mainly the color of my skin and my pink-framed glasses. As someone who believed she was going to have a great first day of preschool, I remember crying on the bus on the way home. All I wanted to do was tell my grandparents I never wanted to go back to that school.

I was the last drop-off for the day and Ms. Margaret, the bus driver, saw my tears and asked if she could walk me to the front door. She took my hand and walked me to the house, where my grandmother, Dorothy, was waiting. My grandmother saw I had been crying and asked Ms. Margaret what happened. Unsure of the story, I remember my grandmother asking Ms. Margaret to see if she could find out. I also recall my grandmother calling her sister-in-law, my Aunt Jill, to get details.

The next day, I did not want to return to preschool, but Ms. Margaret picked me up first and talked to me between stops. Her warmth and reassurance helped me muster my courage. I knew today was going to be a better day in preschool. I got off the bus and walked down the hall with the other children. We got to our rooms and to our assigned seats. This time, my Aunt Jill was in the room and spoke to us about being friends with everyone. As the weeks passed, some of the same children refused to sit by me, or interact with me during art time, but I held on to the friends I did make, and I knew Ms. Margaret would be waiting for me at the end of the school day.

Years later as I entered academia, these feelings of not being included had not changed. My voice was not allowed or appreciated at all conference tables, even though I had the same degrees and sometimes even more experience. I felt like the little Black girl all over again. I needed to find a Ms. Margaret.

My first job was at a midwestern university that was a "primarily white institution." I was in my first year of doctoral studies and was assigned a graduate teaching assistant position, since I have previous teaching experience from a smaller school in the midwest. I clearly remember that first meeting with my supervisor. She was a bit cold and stern, and wanted me to know she was in charge and I would be following her lessons, not developing my own. I worked under her supervision for one academic term. It was awful and I was not sure I wanted to become a professor after all.

For the next semester, I was assigned to another professor, who was absolutely wonderful. From him, I learned so much about the art and love of teaching undergraduate as well as graduate students. He taught me about reflective supervision of my student teachers and backward lesson planning. It was such a change from the last term. I must note that this professor was African American, and he shared with me his own struggles of working at a primarily white institution, and finding and creating our own lane at the university. He taught me about making my space at the table.

Ultimately, I was asked to work with other professors at the university who believed in me and wanted me to excel at my craft. Yet, I constantly struggled and was held to a higher and different standard than my white counterparts. I had to leave my own department of students and teach courses within women's studies and American ethnic studies, in order to gain more experience from seasoned professors of practice.

At the end of this adventure, I did not acquire my doctoral degree, due to multiple issues of racism and sexism. I transferred institutions after completing all of the coursework for my degree. I was heartbroken and felt like the little girl with the pink-framed glasses sitting on the school bus with Ms. Margaret. I missed her words of encouragement and support.

After returning to my home state, I took the plunge and enrolled in another "primarily white institution." I had a history with the university and town, as I had earned my undergraduate degree here. I once again accepted a graduate teaching assistant position, and once again, it was miserable. I did not acquire any substantial research skills. My supervisor made sure my assignments were minimal and tedious, from running her errands to the library or transcribing thousands of hours of documents on a short timeline. I was usually working more than my designated hours and was consistently treated like a child. I needed to find a Ms. Margaret at this institution.

Luckily, I did, and she was able to guide me through four years of my doctoral program to the finish line. My new Ms. Margaret was Ms. Teresa. She believed in me and my knowledge, and above all, expected me to have a seat at the

REASSURANCE

conference table or to build my own table. She guided me on how to handle situations where a seat was not presented to me. She made sure I stood up for myself and that my voice was heard.

I did end up leaving my GTA position at the end of the term, but not without sharing my experience with the department. I was later hired on by the same department in a teaching position. Even though this was a new table, I had to make sure my voice was heard. I was once again met with racist comments during meetings and was asked to be the "spokesperson" for my race. It was not until I left the position a year later that I was asked why I left. I explained that people of color in this position were not treated as equals. Something needed to change. I once again spoke with Ms. Teresa, and she assured me that speaking to the problem and addressing it head on was gaining my seat at the conference table.

I started this story telling you about the little Black girl with the pink-framed glasses who found her space at the art table. I have learned throughout my years in academia and other positions that sometimes it is not about finding your space at the table but building your own table with like-minded individuals, and surrounding yourself with Ms. Margarets and Ms. Teresas who believe in you and see the world through your eyes. Find those individuals who offer support and encouragement for you to create your own truly inclusive spaces.

I am proud of the little Black girl with the pink-framed glasses. She has taught me about myself and self-love and respect. She taught me how to have a wonderful first day sitting at any table.

BRANDY D. JAMES

Brandy D. James, Ph.D., is a director of outreach and education at the University of Arizona. She completed her doctorate in elementary education and specialization in early childhood special education from Ball State University. She is the author of "Makenna the Mighty," a book for families and children experiencing dis/ability and chronic conditions based on her experiences as a mother of a child with dis/abilities. She spent her early career working for Migrant Head Start, Parents as Teachers, and the Girl Scouts Beyond Bars-Kinship programs throughout the Midwest. She holds faculty positions in family studies and early childhood education.

REFLECTION QUESTIONS

1 Ms. Margaret is a central character in Brandy's story. Why do you think that Ms. Margaret was so important to both the young Brandy and adult Brandy? How did the adults in your life support your growing sense of identity as a child?

2 Brandy met issues of racism frequently in her experiences in academia. This is a common problem for Black educators. How have you seen this problem surface in your own life? If you have not seen this happen, why do you think it might be a problem?

3 Have you had a Ms. Margaret in your life? How might you embody Ms. Margaret's care and concern to support someone in your life?

"MY PASSION AS AN EDUCATOR HAS BEEN FUELED BY A LIFELONG COMMITMENT TO ACTIVISM AND SOCIAL JUSTICE."

— RUKIA MONIQUE ROGERS

PASSION
RUKIA MONIQUE ROGERS

I envision a world full of love, empathy, equity, and justice. A world where each human has agency over their body, freedom from harm and the "brutality of capitalism," access to health care, housing, food, and basic rights. Education creates connection between this envisioned world and our daily work and practices. My passion as an educator has been fueled by a lifelong commitment to activism and social justice. My journey has been the collective story of my family and my people, in which education was viewed as the gateway for upward mobility.

My birth was unexpected. My mother was nineteen and approaching her sophomore year of college. She was the first in my entire extended family to have the opportunity to go to college. Dropping out of school was not an option, so my family rallied to support my mother and embrace me with love and devotion. The University of Wisconsin became the backdrop of my early childhood, with the diversity, the freedom, connections to the natural world, and listening to conversations of young Black and brown students wrestling with racism. My mother began engaging me in activism at a young age. I remember her participation in various organizations and pulling me out of school on Dr. Martin Luther King's birthday to participate in a rally demanding a federal holiday in his honor. The early experiences of living in diverse and progressive communities helped to shape my approach to education. Although it took me many years to get there.

I continued to be drawn to politics, campaigning for Carol Mosley Braun (the first Black woman elected to the Senate) in high school. I later declared political science as my major and continued my volunteerism. In the midst of all this, I embarked on a spiritual journey that ultimately led to my conversion to Islam and a new identity as a Black Muslim woman. It again was a new space for me. It was diverse, but there were colliding ideas of old traditions and progressive values.

I began teaching Islamic studies to young children in the mosque. With no formal teacher education, I embarked on innovative ways to work with young children in this context. Pushing back against the traditionalist approaches, I incorporated project work, storying, and singing. My political narrative was ever present. I wanted the children to think and have critical thinking skills. Simultaneously, war was breaking out in the Balkans and I began working with refugees fleeing persecution. I began to wonder, "what if?" What if we invested in young children and their families the way that we invest in war and the military industry? I became more invested in a progressive approach to education. My community noticed my passion and sponsored my formal education. After earning my associate's degree in early childhood education, I worked for several years in mostly affluent Reggio-inspired programs. While

PASSION

I continued to learn and grow as an educator, I yearned for the power to create a space where equity and social justice education thrived. In 2007, I began having conversations with colleagues about the possibilities of opening a progressive preschool. This journey led me to continue to study the educators of Reggio Emilia, New Zealand, the Highlander Folk School and the Civil Rights movement. In 2013, through love, support from a community of fellow educators, and the acquisition of a small business loan, The Highlander School opened its doors.

I would like to think of the creation of The Highlander School as part of an ongoing story. A story that began as a dream for every child, every citizen, to live into his or her fullest potential. With sincere humility, I've often described myself as the "inheritor of this dream," a member of the first generation born after the Civil Rights movement, reaping the benefits of the unrelenting work that my mother, my family, and so many others carried out. Their perseverance was deeply rooted in hope and a desire for a better future for their children. Equity in education was viewed as a cornerstone of progress and a rebuttal of oppression. In this context, I see this chapter of the American story as a parallel to the narrative of the emergence of the municipal infant-toddler centers and preschools of Reggio Emilia, Italy.

The internationally recognized schools of Reggio Emilia arose out of the ashes of World War II, in a country devastated by fascism and conflict. And yet its citizens, with determination and conviction, sought to rebuild, ignited by their aspirations for their children and a vision of a democratic and just society. What truly is an inspiration is the systemic manner in which this community developed schools over the next decades. The educators collaboratively pressed through conflicts to actualize the theories of John Dewey, Paul Hawkins, and the theory of social constructivism from Lev Vygotsky.

These schools were placed on the world stage when, in 1994, a Newsweek article named the schools in Reggio as the best in the world. This attention brought inquisitive educators from around the world, including many from the United States, like myself. Visitors to the early childhood schools of Reggio Emilia are often impressed by the beauty and thoughtfulness of the spaces, the visible traces of the culture, the view of children as highly competent, and their progressive pedagogy. Often in our intrigue and awe of the Reggio educators' work with young children and families, educators have overlooked the rich history and story behind their accomplishments. Our consumption culture, mistakenly, prompted some of us to seek a "how-to" manual.

In 2008, I had the opportunity to visit Reggio Emilia and its infant-toddler and preschool centers to learn—and I'm still learning! I've struggled to describe that experience, as it was so rich and wrapped me in a cascade of thoughts and reflections. Something quite unexpected happened to me in Reggio Emilia. I journeyed there looking for answers and, in turn, they challenged me to look within. Carl Jung's words seemed to resonate more than ever: "He who looks outward dreams. He who looks inward, awakens."

How ironic that I traveled thousands of miles to study the philosophy of the educators of Reggio Emilia, and yet I under-appreciated my own history,

"WHILE I CONTINUED TO LEARN AND GROW AS AN EDUCATOR, I YEARNED FOR THE POWER TO CREATE A SPACE WHERE EQUITY AND SOCIAL JUSTICE EDUCATION THRIVED."

— RUKIA MONIQUE ROGERS

including the fact that I live mere miles from the birthplace of Dr. Martin Luther King and the Civil Rights movement. In pondering this, I found a correlation between the narratives of the schools of Reggio Emilia and those of the Civil Rights movement. Both were communities coming to grips with the reality that all of their citizens were unable to attain life, liberty, and the pursuit of happiness.

In examining my own history, I was inspired by the role of The Highlander Folk School in southern Tennessee. It served as a safe haven for racially integrated dialogue and prepared many leaders in the Southeast, including Dr. King, Rosa Parks, and John Lewis, for non-violent resistance to social injustice.

> "I AM COMMITTED TO CREATING A COMMUNITY OF LEARNERS, BASED UPON THE IDEAS AND VALUES OF DEMOCRACY."
>
> — RUKIA MONIQUE ROGERS

Our new Highlander School for our youngest citizens draws its inspiration from the schools of Reggio and from both civil rights leaders and ordinary citizens who made extraordinary commitments to ensure that everyone has a voice and a seat at the table. Our work in the United States is still incomplete. As my mother would often say, "The dream of Dr. King still won't be fully realized until all children have the same opportunities to receive a decent education."

I am committed to creating a community of learners, based upon the ideas and values of democracy. You won't find worksheets or flashcards at The Highlander School. This is not because we don't want children to learn; in fact, we do! But learning in a democracy is more than just memorization. "To save man from the morass of propaganda, in my opinion, is one of the chief aims of education. Education must enable one to sift and weigh evidence, to discern the true from the false, the real from the unreal, and the facts from the fiction," wrote Dr. King in "The Purpose of Education."

Our endeavor is to continue to foster a community in which children learn how to learn. We want children and citizens to develop critical thinking skills and foster the ability to understand another person's perspective while articulating their own. The Highlander School values children not for their future economic function in society, but for their undeniable right to be in this world as respected citizens here and now.

Our industry still remains a white-centered profession, wherein the dominant theories and organizations are Eurocentric. This reality often places our work in direct conflict with family and community expectations. I, however, continue to remain hopeful, especially as emerging Black and brown voices such as Bettina Love and Beverly Danielle Tatum share insight and new understandings. My story remains the collective tapestry of joy, struggle, and an unwavering belief that we can create a better world.

RUKIA MONIQUE ROGERS

Rukia Monique Rogers has worked with young children and their families for over twenty-five years, including work as a preschool and toddler teacher, a studio teacher, and a curriculum coordinator. In 2013, she founded The Highlander School in Atlanta's greater community, with a rich history to draw on. She is inspired by the educators of Reggio Emilia, by Bettina Love, Dr. Martin Luther King, Jr., and many others who see education as a fundamental right, as well as a catalyst for social change. Rukia is an anti-bias and anti-racist educator committed to cultivating a community full of love.

REFLECTION QUESTIONS

1 Rukia grew up in a college town, surrounded by progressive thinkers in a somewhat tumultuous time in history. How did those early experiences shape her understanding of education and its purpose?

2 When she joined the Nation of Islam, Rukia found her home teaching the children, and generous support from her community to pursue her dream. What stereotypes about Islam have you experienced or held and how does this story counteract them?

3 Throughout the essay we see Rukia grow in her career from a woman who has a passion for educating children to a business owner and respected leader in the field. What qualities do you see in Rukia that might have helped her move through this journey?

"DON'T ALLOW ANYONE TO PLACE A PERIOD WHERE GOD HAS PLACED A COMMA!"

— CRYSTAL SANFORD-BROWN

REBIRTH
CRYSTAL SANFORD-BROWN

Our deepest fear is not that we are inadequate. Our deepest fear is that we are powerful beyond measure. It is our light, not our darkness that most frightens us. We ask ourselves, who am I to be brilliant, gorgeous, talented, fabulous? Actually, who are you not to be? You are a child of God. Your playing small does not serve the world. There is nothing enlightened about shrinking so that other people won't feel insecure around you. We are all meant to shine, as children do. We were born to make manifest the glory of God that is within us. It's not just in some of us; it's in everyone. And as we let our own light shine, we unconsciously give other people permission to do the same. As we are liberated from our own fear, our presence automatically liberates others."
— Marianne Williamson

No more secrets. My experience has been that secrets keep you in a sick state of mind. No longer will I remain silent about my experiences with the internal Black-woman-on-Black-woman conflicts. Yes, out of pain, advances are made. However, during these far too many numerous encounters, I have continually pleaded with God to please make the lessons I'm to learn from the tribulations as clear as possible. No rational person wants to use any portion of their three pounds of brain matter to entertain irrational behavior. Yet, how can we ignore patterns and actions which put us continually under attack? In sharing my experiences with Black-on-Black women attacks, I will focus on encounters that occurred within a higher education institution, which shook the stability of my previously beloved career.

> "I WAS BEING INSTRUCTED BY ANOTHER BLACK WOMAN TO DEVALUE MYSELF AND REMAIN SILENT."
>
> — CRYSTAL SANFORD-BROWN

I'll begin at the beginning. Almost as soon as I began talking, I exhibited a serious speech impediment. Once I began first grade, I received out-of-class support services through a Title I program at my elementary school. By the time I was in the fourth grade, my parents would learn that I also had poor visual acuity, which played a major role in how I saw and heard spoken words.

After I received my first pair of glasses, my ability for higher level thinking quickly fell into place. My teachers began assigning me coursework for high achievers. For years, I questioned if perhaps at least one of my school teachers in my elementary years recognized why I was so frightened when I was called upon. Because I was a victim of childhood sexual abuse at the hands of my aunt and uncle, I had been groomed to be silent.

REBIRTH

At the midpoint of my fifth grade year, school administrators suggested that I be double-promoted to the seventh grade. My parents took into consideration how my sister (who is eleven months and eleven days older than I am), would handle this, and they refused the offer. I continued on my academic journey, becoming one of the first graduates of Renaissance High School in Detroit in 1981. After completing six higher education credentials, I began to realize that I was focusing on my education in order to hide behind the many cut places within my head and heart.

Still remaining silent, at nineteen years of age, I married someone who would repeat the cycle in which he was reared: domestic abuse. My oldest son was born visually impaired due to first trimester abuse and now, as a result, he deals with two lifelong visual conditions. If only I would have left my former husband the very first time he told me, "If you'd only listen to me, then I wouldn't have to beat you. And if you tell any of our friends, no one will believe you!"

My former husband's mother stated in her Patois dialect, "Stand by your man!"

I was being instructed by another Black woman to devalue myself and remain silent.

My experiences navigating my son's therapies and early educational experiences ultimately led me to a full-time career in early childhood. I started dipping my toe in ECE when my daughter was in preschool by offering to care for some of her fellow classmates after school. That turned into a successful family child care in my home. Due to its success, I was approached by my church about opening a center in its facilities.

Following the creation of that program, I went to work in the area of child care resource and referral. While I enjoyed that work, I was paid poorly and not provided with much-needed health, dental, or vision benefits. Instead, the executive director told me that I should access the benefits available through the State of Michigan. I learned from another fellow employee that one of the other few Black females on staff was given the very benefits for herself and her family that I had requested. Yet, I was asked to remain silent about an issue that pitted two Black women against each other due to socio-economic status.

In an act of unexpected but perfect timing, I applied for a full-time position at Oakland Community College, one of the largest community colleges in the state of Michigan, accredited as a state institution of higher education. I took my portfolio in for the interview, and the selection panel was highly impressed. At least ten people were part of my interview process, and ultimately, I was offered the job, which came with a huge salary raise and excellent benefits. I said yes, not even knowing that I could have negotiated my salary.

Once I began the position as a coordinator of the children's center, I realized that I was going to be working with two white female lead early childhood educators. As someone who is accustomed to being the only Black person at many leadership tables, I initially did not see that as a concern. I would be the first, and ultimately the only, Black woman in this position at the closure of all

"... I FINALLY REALIZED
THE ONE THING I HAD BEEN
SEARCHING FOR MY ENTIRE LIFE.
I AM ENOUGH."

— CRYSTAL SANFORD-BROWN

the on-campus children's centers at the end of the fall 2013 semester. They'd never had anyone with credentials in this role. But in this higher education environment, I wasn't prepared for the racism and racist attacks hurled at me, including attacks from Black women.

One of the women I worked with was a prior student of mine. When I walked in, she said with surprise, "You interviewed for this job?"

As it turns out, without the proper credentials, the institution had allowed her to step into the role of the interim coordinator, and she remained possessive of the role. From the start, her attitude was, "This is what we do. We're not looking for any changes."

It did not take long for me to explain, "There's gonna be some changes."

For example, when I first toured the center, I noticed that the teachers had given the children Twizzlers and juice for their snack. They had never made a daily schedule or a nutritious, balanced menu for the week. I knew I needed to establish programs and procedures from the ground up. I began making changes, bringing in conformity, lesson plans, and menus based on the U.S. Department of Education's school food program, in order to meet the dietary needs of the children. I mandated breaks and put policies into place. The institution began to realize that its centers had been seriously out of

> "I WASN'T PREPARED FOR THE RACISM AND RACIST ATTACKS HURLED AT ME, INCLUDING ATTACKS FROM BLACK WOMEN."
>
> — CRYSTAL SANFORD-BROWN

compliance with the state's licensing guidelines. Meantime, my counterparts at the other campuses (four white women) had an attitude of, "Who does she think she is?"

There was hostility. I was on the receiving end of numerous malicious actions. One co-worker would call our licensing consultant with inaccurate information. Her accusations were baseless and I had an impeccable reputation that preceded me, from many years of working in various positions within the field. My main colleague, the former interim coordinator, undermined me with parents, claiming that she was the "real director." Others among my new colleagues, including the Black student workers, were defiant and were directed not to perform any tasks that I may ask of them. After two long years of handling meetings with union representatives, followed up by disciplinary actions, one June day, things changed when she resigned on her lunch break.

Fast forward: I'm coordinator of several of the college's centers by 2013, when I took on a new position as manager of campus affairs, within the campus dean's office. This included some outside networking with the public schools, Rotary clubs, the Chamber of Commerce, and state and city events for neighboring communities. I thoroughly enjoyed my job. I was well respected and good at my position.

Exactly eighteen months after my promotion, there was an opening for a campus dean-level position. I later learned that by following the format of the previous manager of campus affairs, who aspired to become a dean,

I was already doing the tasks of a dean. Several of us in administration positions applied. Early childhood education was one of the institution's highest graduating disciplines, but I believe the college devalued the field—our own students didn't even do their internships in our on-campus centers.

Ultimately, I was told I didn't meet the criteria for the dean's position because I hadn't worked for student services long enough, and my eight years of ECE administration experience didn't count because "it was just babysitting." The selected campus deans would commence their new roles during the first week of October 2014. This would also be the time when my mom would relocate to a new residence. The move, which should have only taken two or three days, took nearly a week. At the time of my Dad's death, my parents had been married forty-seven years, and there's no doubt in my mind that my Mom had mementos from each of these years! With just a small amount of assistance from the grandchildren, I solely assisted my mom in this move.

When I submitted an emergency request for time off, my new supervisor went ballistic! She accused me of taking time off at the onset of her role as the campus dean, stating that I knew that I was supposed to train her for her position. When I explained the urgency to assist my mom, she failed to believe me.

This would be the second incident of harassment. The initial incident occurred while she was still in her previous position, and had single-handedly rescheduled a new student orientation for an evening when I was scheduled to teach at another campus. None of the other administrators involved with these orientations would be available either. Prior to my departure, I assured my administrative staff that all materials and the support of one student ambassador were in place for the extremely small number of students who had registered to attend this orientation. During my drive to instruct, my colleague continually contacted me on cell, insisting that I cancel my class for the evening and return to assist her. I refused, and fulfilled my commitment to instruct that evening.

Shortly thereafter, this colleague began to harass my staff while calling me a stupid "B." I reported the incident to the campus administration, which resulted in a meeting. This colleague denied making the disparaging remarks to my staff about me, then as we were exiting the meeting, she said, "You should have remained silent. We could have worked through your concerns on our own!" I totally disagreed.

Those two incidents would be the onset of two LONG years of working in a toxic work environment. That era impacted my physical and my mental health. Through that experience, I was diagnosed with anxiety, stress, and post-traumatic stress disorder. The incidents I experienced ultimately triggered trauma from my past, when I had been conditioned to accept abuse.

At her worst, this colleague would come into my office, close the doors, and hurl accusations and insults at me.

"I don't know why you're telling on me. No one will believe you."

"I know you don't respect me, but you'll learn to respect me."

"You will eventually get down to a size five once you start running after me."

"I don't know why you're getting a doctorate degree; I'm still going to be over you."

"I've decided that you will no longer represent the college in the community because you eat too much."

"Can you fix your skirt, I'm sick of looking at the zipper on the wrong area of your butt."

This was just a sampling of her egregious behavior. She stalked me on social media. She would come into my office and demand that I listen to her racist comments about one of the white female deans that she knew I was friendly with. This was a living hell!

The situation, and my health, devolved so much that I asked for a transfer. Human resources and the institution's attorney allowed a transfer. Six months later, I received notification via email just before the holiday break, to report back to that toxic workplace upon the institution's reopening in early January. The leadership had decided that just asking this woman not to speak to me would suffice.

REBIRTH

Instead, she continually body shamed me, religion shamed me, stole my documents from the master printer in the suite—it was endless. Additionally, I was in a doctoral program, and had class at 6 p.m. on Fridays in a different city. My colleague would deliberately call meetings on Fridays at 5 p.m., knowing that I had to leave and that technically my workday was complete. When I tried desperately to explain my situation to leadership, a common response was, "You're two Black women." There was an implication that we should just work things out. I was told to let her abusive behavior run off my back like water off a duck's feathers.

"You just have different personality styles. Just ignore her."

Finally, in early February 2017, after I burst a blood vessel in my eye, my doctor said, "Get out of there before you have a stroke or a heart attack." I was making an excellent salary, but I knew I had to leave.

As a faith believer, I was given numerous signs that my given assignment had been completed, yet I tried everything I could to hold onto the job while God was placing one challenge after another in my path, signaling a need for my exodus. Once I could no longer physically or mentally continue to work in such a toxic environment, I left my beloved job.

Don't allow one to place a period where God has placed a comma! Within a short span of time, blessings started coming. One after another. Did you know that the number 8 is the symbol of harmony and represents the ability to make decisions and new beginnings? In 2018, at the age of fifty-five, during a presentation to the attendees at the annual Oakland County Child Care Council provider appreciation brunch, I received the power of God as I would, for the very first time, publicly share that I had been diagnosed with PTSD. My PTSD stemmed from being molested as a child by relatives, the domestic abuse in my marriage, several unhealthy relationships, and working in an extremely toxic environment. While I continually achieved educationally over the years, I held deep, dark secrets that kept me hostage to my shame.

> "IN THAT MOMENT, NO ONE COULD TELL ME THAT I WASN'T SMART ENOUGH OR STRONG ENOUGH OR WORTHY ENOUGH."
>
> — CRYSTAL SANFORD-BROWN

In June of 2018, I reached a major milestone in my life and started my four-year term as the vice president of the governing board for the National Association for the Education of Young Children. In December of that year, this brown-eyed little girl from Detroit, who previously stuttered and carried the shame and ill secrets of adults, had a life-altering experience: on the behalf of NAEYC, I traveled to Hangzhou, China to present two seminars at China's largest early childhood conference with over 17,000 attendees. I had phenomenal individuals who translated my words into the Mandarin language. It felt like a powerful culmination of my life's work. In that moment, no one could tell me that I wasn't smart enough or strong enough or worthy enough. Standing on that stage in front of thousands of faces I finally realized the one thing I had been searching for my entire life. I am enough.

After forgiving the ill behavior of relatives who preyed upon me, I gave my

REBIRTH

vow to God. I vowed to God that I would devote the remainder of my life to advocating for young people who are impacted by adverse childhood experiences, or ACES. In 2019, that vow became a reality when I founded Emerging Young Leadership, Inc. To date, we have supported hundreds of students, families, and loved ones, in order to foster a new generation of leaders who have overcome significant challenges in their own lives. I've learned many valuable lessons from my experiences:

- You can't bring out of people what's not in them. An apology was nowhere in my supervisor's vocabulary, or consciousness.
- Through challenges, and during disequilibrium, we learn best.
- Foster an inner circle of colleagues and friends you can always trust.
- Don't hold onto vengeance.

Your aspirations, desires, dreams, and hopes are waiting for you. The seeds of your future have been planted, so that you may flourish and pay it forward. I became more encouraged, empowered and enlightened as a result of an ordeal that nearly tore me to pieces. And it wasn't my struggle. It didn't belong to me. It belonged to my colleague, but I carried the silence far too long!

CRYSTAL SANFORD-BROWN

Crystal Sanford-Brown, recently retired, is a seasoned early childhood advocate within the early childhood field. Having served in direct care as a licensed facilitator of family and group child care homes, a child care center owner, and an early childhood resource and referral specialist, she celebrated more than ten years as a coordinator of on-campus children's centers. Crystal continues to highlight the importance of quality early childhood education and environments for young children.

REFLECTION QUESTIONS

1 Crystal found leadership opportunities in both her state and national early childhood associations. In her state organization, she was the first Black president in history. Reflect on your own experiences in early childhood groups that you belong to. How diverse are they? What could you do to help not only bring diverse people to the table, but also create spaces where they are truly included?

2 While working at the community college, Crystal was bullied by someone in leadership who happened to be another Black woman. Many women have had both positive and negative experiences with female bosses. Why do you think these relationships can be tricky? How would you have responded to the situation?

3 Adverse Childhood Experiences (ACEs) are central to Crystal's story and her work today. What is your role in understanding the ACEs that others might have experienced? How can you help those who have been silenced by trauma find their voice?

For more information on Crystal's organization, Emerging Youth Leadership, Inc., please visit emergingyl.org. Domestic abuse is a serious problem. If you or someone you know is being abused, contact the National Domestic Abuse Violence Hotline at 1-800-799-7233

"... I WONDER IF THEY SEE ALL OF ME OR JUST THE PARTS THAT RUN COUNTER TO WHAT THEY EXPECTED."

— MEGHAN L. GREEN

INTERSECTIONALITY
MEGHAN L. GREEN

How did I get to where I am today? My answer may seem convoluted, but the truth is that I think I was always meant to facilitate the co-construction of knowledge with young children. I am from a small town in southwest Louisiana and the product of two generations of educators. My belief in the importance of education is coupled with my resolute belief in its power. Through my firsthand experiences and those of my family members, I have witnessed the changes that education can make in one's life.

My first memories of learning as a young child include the smell of freshly cut sugarcane wafting into the open windows of the large one room schoolhouse, which had been built by my great grandfather and other Black sharecroppers in 1921. Generations of my kin created the foundation for educational attainment and leadership in what is now the only surviving Rosenwald Foundation school in Louisiana. In tandem, my formal educational experiences have given me the chance to meet some of the greatest minds of our time. Growing up in my family, there were three career choices for intelligent Black children: doctor, lawyer, or teacher. I knew early on that I wanted to travel a different route. My undergraduate major, anthropology, could have easily prepared me for any of these noble professions, but after much consideration I found myself drawn to one. Teaching was the keystone to life, or so my grandmother believed, and it became the way in which I shared my gift with the world.

Despite my thirteen years of experience, I am often met with stares when I walk into a room of early childhood professionals. The reactions of others to my presence normally fall into one of several categories: 1) "Who is she?"; 2) "Why does she look like that?"; 3) "I wonder what she does here."

I have always struggled with balancing the disconnect between my perceived identity and my actual identity. When most people see me, I wonder if they see all of me or just the parts that run counter to what they expected. My outward appearance may give people the impression that my life contains certain elements. Those elements may include a collection of lifestyles: being a mother, being a student, being a daughter, or half-dozen other identity markers that people commonly associate with my appearance. I have this natural hair, these tattoos, and these huge earrings that people love to comment on.

The conversations I have with white folks about the meaning or symbolism behind my physical identity markers are very different from the conversations I have with Black people about the symbols on my body. When white people encounter my body adornments in professional settings, they often ask questions that unmask their process of reconciling who they think I am against who I assert I am.

INTERSECTIONALITY

"Is that Africa on your earrings?" "How do you manage to do everything that you do?" "Where did you grow up?" "Are you worried about what parents think of you?"

Encounters with Black folks stand in direct opposition, however. I was once at a graduate student reception at an educational research conference and I remember sitting at a table and having one of the other Black graduate students ask me about the tattoo of an Adinkra symbol on my left wrist. He asked me if I knew what the symbol meant. I explained to him that I did, and then proceeded to tell him the meaning it held for me and why I wanted it permanently placed on my body in the first place. He then shared with me that the symbol was part of his cultural heritage. His family was part of the Adinkra cultural group in Ghana. I was honored that he took those moments to ensure that I was not blindly appropriating his family's cultural representation.

The most poignant example of the dissonance between my perceived identity and my actual identity stems from trainings I have facilitated at early childhood education conferences across the country. My routine when setting up for a training has not wavered for the past few years. I begin by queuing up the slide presentation to display my title slide on the screen. The title of the training, my name, and my educational accolades are all prominently displayed, but my photo is noticeably absent. As participants enter the room, I often overhear discussions about how the title piques their interest and their thoughts on the potential content for the session. Then, as if prompted by an invisible source, I hear a familiar refrain from somewhere in the room, "I wonder who the presenter is. I am not acquainted with them."

That comment always makes me think about how people's implicit bias complicates their attempt to place me into a neat little box just based on my name. It is a lesson on observing anti-bias education in action, unfolding as the participants enter a space focused on examining the role of implicit bias in our interactions with the children and families. The people that I am about to spend the next ninety minutes with discussing definitions and textbook examples of implicit bias never stop to think how their behavior in the moments leading up to the start of the training is an example of this very topic.

After collecting my thoughts, I walk to the front of the room and introduce myself. "Welcome everyone! My name is Meghan L. Green, and we will be sharing this space together to analyze how implicit bias impacts how we interact with children and families as early childhood educators."

I tend to begin the session with a story of how my family and I have been affected by other people's implicit bias. For example, I remember beginning a session with a narrative about my youngest son's most poignant encounter with racism. When he was in pre-kindergarten at the child care center at my university, one of his white peers told him that he did not want to play with him because he was Black. His teachers and the director of the center were typical well-meaning white folks. They apologized profusely and assured me that they would speak to the other child's parents. They spent more time trying to convince me of their "good" intentions than they did addressing the impact that situation had on my son.

"HOW DO I LIMIT THE IMPACT THAT OTHER PEOPLE'S PERCEPTIONS OF ME HAVE ON HOW I SHOW UP IN THE WORLD?"

— MEGHAN L. GREEN

The story I choose to share with each group is based on the energy that I feel in the room. I use multiple examples because I enjoy showing the intersections of my identity. There are so many ways in which I move in this world, and each intersection presents a new set of challenges to or opportunities for connection. I think that is why Paul Laurence Dunbar's "We Wear the Mask" has always resonated with me. I have always felt as if people are meeting parts of me, as opposed to all of me. My life seems to have always been this game of people trying to decipher between the version of me they think they are interacting with and the version of me they are actually interacting with.

> "THERE ARE SO MANY WAYS IN WHICH I MOVE IN THIS WORLD, AND EACH INTERSECTION PRESENTS A NEW SET OF CHALLENGES TO OR OPPORTUNITIES FOR CONNECTION."
>
> — MEGHAN L. GREEN

Early on, I learned that I felt safer when I was able to limit people's access to certain parts of me. This defense mechanism was a result of experiencing how people sifted through my identities to find the ones that made them most comfortable. Black. Queer. Femme. They often disregarded the parts of me that made them question their long-standing beliefs. I always felt hurt in those instances, in which those around me felt positively about one part of my identity, but did not bring that same energy when interacting with other parts.

I felt this simultaneous space of otherness most pointedly in 2018, while I was campaigning for the student representative seat on the governing

INTERSECTIONALITY

board of the National Association for Education of Young Children. It is customary for governing board candidates to interact with members during the organization's annual conference in the fall. Our schedules over that week are packed with opportunities to visit interest forums' business meetings to talk to members about their concerns regarding the organization. This was only my second year attending NAEYC's annual conference, and I was excited at the prospect of representing early childhood educators from multiple marginalized communities. I attended several events hosted by the Black Caucus and was welcomed as a Black mother and an educator. The discussions in these meetings centered around NAEYC's commitment to Black children's academic, social, and emotional well-being. I was able to provide insight into my experiences as the single, working mother of two Black boys. That perspective was safe to those around me. Most of my peers in those spaces were unaware of my sexual identity, so when questions about intersectionality arose, no one thought to ask what my opinions might be. I felt like a part of me had been rendered invisible in such a heteronormative space.

The next day, I attended a very meaningful event hosted by the LGBTQ interest forum. I had attended this interest forum's business meeting the previous year and looked forward to seeing a few familiar faces. "A Time for Ourselves" is a very special event hosted by the LGBTQ interest forum every year. During this three-hour session, presenters create a safe space for queer conference attendees to unwind, build community with each other, and discuss strategies for supporting LGBTQ early childhood educators. While allies are welcome to attend the session in support, they must do so with the understanding that their voices are not centered.

I could not wait to attend this session as both a participant and a governing board candidate. My candidacy represented the intersections of multiple identities that are often marginalized in professional early childhood education spaces, and I wanted to share this hopeful news with those in my community. As I walked into the crowded room, I noticed something strange: I was one of perhaps two or three queer people of color and maybe the only Black queer woman in the session. That familiar feeling of "outsider" began to creep into my chest, and not even the big blue button reading "NAEYC Governing Board Candidate" could make me feel more seen. I quickly found a seat at the table and introduced myself to a few folks around me. We talked about our sexual and gender identities and how they impacted our professional lives. I made it a point to discuss how my identity as a pansexual femme presenting woman also impacted how I moved as a Black woman in early childhood spaces. In this session, my sexual identity was a common source of marginalization, but my race was barely mentioned. This space with my white LGBTQ peers felt more like home, while still missing elements of the depth I experienced in the Black-centered spaces at the conference.

All these experiences leave me to ponder the following question: How do I limit the impact that other peoples' perceptions of me have on how I show up in the world? My spheres of identity are plentiful, ranging from Black to queer to female. The labels I ascribe to myself give a context for my beliefs and actions. In various contexts, I have occupied the space of "other" my entire life. This identity crisis is what prompted my entrance into the discipline of early childhood education. I wanted to use my ability to move fluidly between worlds based on my race, gender, and sexual orientation. My desire to end systems of oppression through the vehicle of education is rooted in my early educational experiences as the perceived exception to society's rules. The fallacy of the token "other" in American society can be explained when I consider how the intersections of my life have shaped how I interact with the world. As an early childhood educator and anti-racist training facilitator, I strive to create educational and professional spaces for the folks who live and love as I do. Audre Lorde once asserted that "if I didn't define myself for myself, I would be crunched into other people's fantasies for me and eaten alive." Her words provide the requisites for liberation through self-awareness and offer folks like me solace and comfort as we seek to change the world around us as perpetual outsiders. How did I get to where I am now? I made it here by constantly defining and redefining who I am on my own terms.

MEGHAN L. GREEN

Meghan L. Green, M.Ed., is a fourth grade teacher at Uplift Ascend Primary in Fort Worth, Texas as well as an adjunct professor of early childhood studies at the University of North Texas. She is also currently a doctoral candidate studying curriculum and instruction with a specialization in early childhood education at Texas A&M University-Commerce. Ms. Green earned her bachelor's degree in anthropology with a minor in African American studies from Howard University and a master's of education in early childhood education from Northwestern State University. Ms. Green's scholarship centers Black feminist thought within early childhood settings.

REFLECTION QUESTIONS

1 Meghan shares with us how she is regularly confronted with the expectations of others, due to their implicit biases. How do you think that others' perceptions of you have either negatively or positively affected your career path?

2 The first goal of anti-bias education focused on identity. How have Meghan's own personal identities supported her work as an educator?

3 Take time to unpack your identities and make some commitments to show up as your own, authentic self in your work.

4 Meghan's story celebrates times of being fully seen and creating safe spaces for others. When have you experienced being fully seen? What are some safe spaces for you?

"I WAS ALSO REMINDED THAT CULTURE IS AT THE CENTER OF THE WORK I DO AS AN EDUCATOR, AND THAT KNOWING MYSELF IS ONE OF THE MOST IMPORTANT PIECES."

— OLGA LACAYO

RESOLUTE
OLGA LACAYO

I was not meant to be here telling my story, but the universe conspired, along with my courageous ancestors, to make it happen through their bravery and love of life.

I am a Garifuna, born and raised in a picturesque, remote Garifunan village bathed by the warm waters of the Caribbean Sea on the north coast of Honduras in Central America. My Garifuna village was the perfect setting for childhood. My resilience and resolve to keep reinventing myself are a testament to the Garifunans' greatness and resolve to overcome their turbulent past and forge a new path. This is a path that we Garifuna are still walking today.

The Garifuna originated on the island of Saint Vincent from the fusion of Carib Indians and Indian Arawak. Their ancestors were enslaved Africans brought to the Caribbean islands to work on the sugar cane plantations in the mid-1600s. It is believed that the ship carrying them either shipwrecked in a storm or they took over once they sailed close to the shores of the

Caribbean islands. They made it to the shores of Saint Vincent and made it their home, until 1763 when the Europeans signed a treaty that gave the island to the British Empire. Since such treaties did not offer a guarantee of total control of the island, the British battled the Garifuna over the control of the island until 1797, when the Garifuna finally surrendered.

After surrendering, the Garifuna were divided based on the shade of skin color. Over 5,000 of the Garifuna with darker skin were captured, exiled, and held hostage in the rocky and inhospitable island of Balliceaux, where the British allowed them to perish from malnutrition and disease. Half of the Garifuna exiled to Balliceaux died, and some jumped off the rocky cliffs to their death, instead of being subjugated by the British.

On March 11, 1797, the surviving Garifuna people were once again reminded of the middle passage when they were exiled to the Island of Roatan, Honduras. Soon after their arrival, conditions on the island became unsustainable, forcing the Garifuna to relocate to the coasts of Honduras, Belize, Nicaragua, and Guatemala, which have been home to the Garifuna ever since.

There are currently around 700,000 Garinagu living around the world. The Garifuna tapestry includes the Garifuna language, rich gastronomy, spirituality, music, and dance. In 2001, Garifunan music and dance were added to UNESCO's Representative List of the Intangible Cultural Heritage of Humanity. We are people of peace, maybe because of our collective memory of our freedom and peace-loving ancestors. Today, we are still Garifuna regardless of our turbulent history, only thanks to the acts of bravery of our courageous ancestors, who fought valiantly to live and remain Garifuna. Just like my ancestors were not meant to live, I was not meant to be a teacher. However, just as they broke the bondage that was imposed on them from the very beginning of their existence, I resisted a system that denied me and my siblings the most basic fundamental rights to an education. My decision to become a teacher was an act of defiance against that system, and my attempt to correct the wrongs and advocate for a more inclusive school system, that welcomes and celebrates diversity.

I first entered a classroom with my older sister, Julia Martinzed, in 1971 in my beloved town of Limón Colón in Honduras. I was not officially enrolled in school because I did not meet the seven years required to enter the education system at that time, but I could go as a listener. I quickly adapted to the routine. I arrived at school on time, I did the homework, I participated in activities with great enthusiasm. In a short time, I was one of the favorite pupils of the teachers because my sisters, brothers, and I already knew how to read and write before entering school. Therefore, the school was like an extension of what we already knew from home and that pleased the teachers. This made my first educational experiences away from home moments that I remember with great regard, and at the same time melancholy, due to what took place almost immediately after that short magic first year.

My parents were very hardworking people: well-respected in the community, dedicated to their family, very disciplined, people of faith. They always thought that education started at home and they undertook this endeavor with rigor. We did not participate fully in most of the events of the town, but that did not affect me in any way, from my child's point of view. Life went on, my childhood was the happiest. I had the unconditional love of my parents, my cousins, grandparents, neighbors, and friends. We were a big happy family and we had everything we needed, emotionally, materially, and spiritually.

My father worked in the banana fields for many years, a job of much "prestige" for a Garifuna at that time. This allowed him to save some of his salary and then return to his village and establish his own food market and hospitality business, which was very successful. My father was a pioneer, he was a humanitarian, and he never denied help to those in need. I have beautiful memories of my childhood. People from many places and from different walks of life came to my house. I remember with fondness the exchanges and the attention they received from my parents, and how they viewed my parents with admiration and respect. Those were indeed the best years of my life and I think that is when I decided that I wanted to serve people.

It was the month of the national independence celebrations and all the students were expected to participate in the parades, parties, and other such celebrations. My brothers and cousins did not participate in the celebrations, consequently, they were permanently banned [expelled] from school and never allowed back. They would serve as an example to all those who wanted to follow their example of "disrespecting the country."

> "I HAVE BEAUTIFUL MEMORIES OF MY CHILDHOOD. PEOPLE FROM MANY PLACES AND FROM DIFFERENT WALKS OF LIFE CAME TO MY HOUSE."
>
> — OLGA LACAYO

RESOLUTE

That experience marked my life and that of my brothers forever. The intolerance, repudiation, mockery, and oppression we were subjected to had no equal. It was the first and last time to this day that something like that happened in the history of Limón Colón. It has been over forty-five years since that bleak September 15th, but the devastation I saw in the eyes of my brothers and cousins still torments me, especially now that I have a clearer understanding of the effects that an event of such magnitude can have on the healthy development of the psyche of a child.

My father was not going to allow his sons and daughters to be humiliated again. He developed a plan to continue to educate us at home. The plan was successful to some degree, because we were already used to it. I enjoyed my studies at home, and we were honestly doing better than most of our friends who were attending school. Some years elapsed, and although we were not completely detached from our community, I felt that I lost a lot in the course of those six or seven years. After we were denied one of the most basic human rights, the right to an education in our own town, my parents basically built a wall around us. I know that they did it with the best of intentions, to protect us from humiliation, but they also hurt us greatly in the process, by limiting our contact with everything, including our Garifuna culture.

My grandfather was instrumental in my enculturation and I will live eternally grateful to him for instilling in me the love for my culture. I remember those years of my childhood with deep love. Those deeply rooted teachings are a constant companion to me as I navigate life. My grandfather's style of education was through oral tradition. He was an avid storyteller. I remember with fondness when he used to gather me and my friends to tell us endless stories on moonlit summer nights; him sitting at the top of the stairs and us the children at the bottom. He would usually start by saying, "Darahumeitia harihei mabuliedahumamugai le narinagubei hun laduga ubati tidan liburu." (Open your ears so you won't forget what I will say, because it is not written in books.) My grandpa never grew tired of teaching me and my friends values such as respect, solidarity, tolerance, integrity, unity, and perseverance through his stories.

My parents did not fight for our right to an education or their right to practice their beliefs and be conscientious objectors. Nor did they fight so that their children were not victimized or discriminated against for something over which they had no control, or the values that were instilled at home. From my perspective, that was a serious mistake. They did not think about the repercussions of their decision to not correct the injustice committed against my brothers and me.

Six years later, in 1976, is when my resistance officially began, without the knowledge of my parents. I was just twelve years old. I credit my brother-in-law, Celestino Bermudez Castro, for giving me the key that for the last forty years has opened many doors for me. He was the husband of one of my cousins, who was also expelled from school that dreadful September 15, 1970. On one of my afternoon visits with my cousin, she shared with me that her husband would help her and some other girls with a few classes to finish elementary school. I told my cousin that I also wanted to receive classes and I asked her if she could help me convince her husband to add me to the group. She agreed. I talked to the school principal, who by now was a Garifuna, and he agreed. I made the arrangement without the knowledge of my parents. I was the first one in my family to finish primary education and consequently upper secondary education. My brothers and cousins followed my example; armed with courage, they all did the same. A total of seven of them completed their primary education, and some of them succeeded in completing higher studies.

As an act of defiance, instead of pursuing a career in psychology as originally planned, I decided that I would be a teacher. I studied teaching at La Escuela Normal Mixta de Trujillo, from which I earned a teaching degree in elementary education in 1986, eight years after I decided to resist the oppression of school authorities and my parents. Years later in 1987, I returned to my hometown, as a professional in elementary school education. With the help of my father, I got a temporary position as a primary school teacher and middle school history teacher in the same school from which my family and I had been expelled. The person who expelled us became my boss until I emigrated to the United States in 1991.

It is undeniable that my parents did an extraordinary job in our upbringing by teaching us universal values about tolerance, integrity, hard work, unconditional love for others, and forgiving others' faults. These values continue to govern my life and are something that I treasure, as I continue to resist and keep walking in what I call my restorative justice. Until recently, I was ashamed to tell the story of how my primary education went, and why I became a teacher. This is the first time that I have armed myself with courage to capture that experience and put it on paper, therefore sharing it with others. Needless to say, for the first time I feel finally released after more than forty-five years. The time is right as I strive to be authentic.

I firmly believe that only by examining myself very deeply, facing my fears, being vulnerable and sharing with people who also have a story to tell can I be successful in this path of transformation that I have begun. I echo the words of one of my favorite authors, Brené Brown, "Today, instead of sitting on the bench and dedicating myself to judge and give advice, I dare to show my face and let myself be seen for what I am, a woman with merit."

> "I FIRMLY BELIEVE THAT ONLY BY EXAMINING MYSELF VERY DEEPLY, FACING MY FEARS, BEING VULNERABLE AND SHARING WITH PEOPLE WHO ALSO HAVE A STORY TO TELL CAN I BE SUCCESSFUL IN THIS PATH OF TRANSFORMATION ..."
>
> — OLGA LACAYO

My thirty-five years in education have been a long, amazing journey, through which I have met wonderful fellow travelers and outstanding guides who took me by the hand and nurtured the wounded but not defeated warrior in me. I have had different significant roles in the twenty-six years since I emigrated to the United States. The most significant role, after being a mother, was, and still is, being a student. Being a student gave me access to people that, just like me, were immigrants and educators who also have stories to tell. It allowed me to surround myself with educators and leaders that champion equity work in education and understand the power of the holistic nature of transformative classrooms.

It was the birth of my children that introduced me to the fascinating world of early childhood education. I vividly remember entering our pediatrician's office one cold November morning with my son, Walter, for his well-baby check. Walter was a very active child. I was a new mother and I had many questions about his development. The doctor was impressed by my inquiry and she not only responded to my questions, she shared that her best friend was the department chair of the child development and family studies of San Francisco City College and that they offered wonderful child observation classes that could benefit Walter and I.

I attended my first child observation class in January of 1993. Since it was the beginning of spring semester, I was able to add some core courses in early childhood education. I was awestruck by what I was learning and I was eager to know and do more. The same instructor teaching the observation class was my first ECE instructor. That was a new beginning for me.

In December of 1993, I accepted a job as an emergency preschool teacher with the child development and family studies department of San Francisco City College. A few years went by and my excitement faded away. I was confronted with the grim reality of being absorbed into an environment where I felt I could not live up to my potential. I was unhappy and I considered quitting. I felt I was not being effective. I did not have a voice. I felt I was not able to build an inclusive classroom, one that was representative of my community and my philosophy as an activist teacher. These were hard times of deep reflection for me. I had to make some very important decisions. I needed to find my way back to the original reasons I became an educator. By becoming a teacher, I wanted to undo the wrong done to me and my family, by creating and supporting an environment in which being different is viewed as an opportunity to create a stronger community, not to harm. I strive to do that by working continuously and diligently to understand and honor the set of values and beliefs that children and their families bring into the classroom, which benefits all participants as we work together to create a vibrant and strong community. Having that as a constant reminder helps me to be aware of how I approach families and student teachers, how I ask questions, how I receive and respond to the information/answers I get, and how I incorporate family contributions into our classroom.

After years of reflecting, digging, and gathering strength, I reached out for support from amazing educators, administrators, and colleagues. A meeting with Dr. Sharon Cronin made me want to advance my education and refocus my work on social justice in ECE. She introduced me to equity work in education through the Soy Bilingue/Dual Language program, and since then, my professional life had not been the same.

Through Soy Bilingue, I was reintroduced to the work of Pablo Freire and was introduced to the work of Dr. Cronin, Dr. Antonia Darder, bell hooks, Louise Derman-Sparks, Augusto Boal, and many other amazing educators, activists, and theorists. Most importantly, I was reintroduced to Olga. I was also reminded that culture is at the center of the work I do as an educator, and that knowing myself is one of the most important pieces, especially when venturing into the deep waters of equity work in a place with people who do not remotely look like me. Our own Soy Bilingue and Seattle EDU classroom became what bell hooks describes as a place that embraces the progressive notion of engaged pedagogy.

> "When education is the practice of freedom, students are not the only ones who are asked to share, to confess. Engaged pedagogy does not seek simply to empower students. Any classroom that employs a holistic model of learning will also be a place where teachers grow and are empowered by the process. That empowerment cannot happen if we refuse to be vulnerable while encouraging students to take risks... When professors bring narratives of their experiences into classroom discussions, it eliminates the possibility that we can function as all knowing, silent interrogators."
> — bell hooks, Teaching to Transgress: Education as the Practice of Freedom, 1994.

After my work with Dr. Cronin, I made the conscious effort to surround myself with supportive and committed educators who also see early childhood as a perfect setting for social justice work. These mentors and colleagues have supported me and have helped me renew my commitment to supporting the next generation of children, parents, ECE students, and educators.

The unique opportunity to be part of Soy Bilingue, and the profound effect it had on me, changed the trajectory of my professional life. It was a transformative experience in the sense that for the first time in my life, I was compelled to share personal experiences with a group of people with which I have a lot in common. It was a safe place to share and examine my own life. All of us in the classroom came to be a living proof of self and social transformation. As students, we were taking control of our lives, getting to know ourselves, and could share our feelings with others without fear of being judged. This was the beginning of my transformation and it was liberating; it was the first time I understood the difference between fitting in and belonging. Sharing and looking closely at our culture, our lives, and society was so transforming for me, there was no looking back.

Before this life-altering experience, I had never in my entire life seen a book, heard a story, a song or a Garifuna poem in a classroom, either in Honduras or the U.S. I had never had an in-depth discussion about Garifuna, their history, who they are and their contributions to the country. Throughout my schooling, the identity of the Garifuna was totally neglected by education officials, even when most of the time the teachers in the Garifuna villages were Garifuna. The language, history, spirituality, and other aspects of the Garifuna culture were never given the attention they deserved. The result of this phenomenon has been devastating for the Garifuna in the form of an unprecedented identity crisis.

Our Soy Bilingue classroom was full of "human knowledge"—people of color coming together who have struggled to assert themselves in a place where we were outsiders, voiceless individuals that must conform to the dictates of others. We all needed to be heard and supported by people who understood the struggle and were willing to guide us to find our voices.

RESOLUTE

Being vulnerable was something new to me, however, knowing that I was not the only one struggling to share stories of struggles and survival, allowed me to open and start the healing process. Now I continue to share experiences. I am surprised to find out that what I thought was going to be an embarrassment, is an inspiration to others. I feel liberated and empowered. I am committed to continue this journey of self-discovery to see where it leads me.

As a Garifuna educator, I have always wondered what kept me strong throughout the years. I categorically believe it was the reality that an entire village took part in keeping me intact. My intent with telling my story is to emphasize the importance of having a strong foundation from early on. I am a testament to the far-reaching impacts that positive experiences have on the development of a child's healthy sense of self. Such experiences have served as shelter against the blows life has sent my way. Being gifted the opportunity to add my story to this anthology is an honor and I am grateful for it. I want to add my voice to that of many educators that do not just want to fit in, but want to belong. We have important stories to tell. Our stories have been and continue to be lost because we were not offered a seat at the table.

OLGA LACAYO

Olga Lacayo has more than thirty-five years of experience in the education field; twenty-eight in early education with City College of San Francisco, including work as a preschool teacher, ECE student's classroom coach, and adult educator. She offers technical assistance and conducts equity driven training for early education teachers and is a professional learning community facilitator. Lacayo has a master's degree in education with concentration in dual language and a bachelor's degree in child and adolescent development with emphasis on children and families. As an educator, she values safe and courageous spaces for students to develop curiosity, explore, flourish, and prosper. Lacayo encourages adults to listen, question, learn, and act to break the silence around bias and racism in the ECE classroom. She believes ECE teachers' empowered voices are essential in working for more equitable classrooms where children are protected from the damaging impact of racial prejudice.

REFLECTION QUESTIONS

1 Olga begins her story with the history of the Garifuna people. How do you think her connection to her culture sustained her through years of setbacks and hard work?

2 Even though Olga had a traumatic experience early in her schooing, she continued to be passionate about education. What role did her family play in helping her to persevere?

3 The Soy Bilingue school was a place where Olga found acceptance and inclusion. How can early educators offer an environment in their programs where all children, families, and educators feel safe and accepted?

"I AM A PEDAGOGICAL LEADER,
A GATE-OPENER,
A SYSTEM CHANGER,
A PROVOCATEUR,
AND A CHANGE AGENT."

— KELLY RAMSEY

PLANTED
KELLY RAMSEY

I am ... a descendent from a proud people rooted in social justice and servant leadership.

I am from the Bay Area: Berkeley, San Francisco, and Oakland, California are the roots that raised me. My ancestors were rooted in the Chickasha, Oklahoma, Bakersfield, California, Houston, and Waxahachi, Texas lands.

I am from the African-American culture, Cherokee nation, French, and Blackfoot Indigenous people.

I am filled with verbal storytelling traditions, foods made from scratch and filled with love, evening dialogue with everyone represented, kitchen chatter in the background, deep discussions in the foreground, children playing board games in the midst.

I am an English language speaker.

KELLY RAMSEY

I am the experience of a home life nurtured by both father and mother, a young married girl, identity shattered, divorcee, broken and healed, restored hope, second marriage, pregnant with joy, broken with despair in miscarriage, healed and restored, pregnant with exuberant joy carrying a son, and another, my legacy living forward.

I am nourished by healthy meals from the garden, planted with our hands, tilled with our hands, brought forth with labor, and cooked with love. Fresh tomatoes, okra, green beans, calabaza squash with onions and peppers, spinach, cantaloupe, collard greens, and black-eyed peas. The family table; restored and enjoyed by all who stop by.

I am a child that emerged from playing outdoors till the street lights went out, exploring our town, riding bikes in the streets, visiting the public library, riding the city bus in the summertime, climbing trees and picking fruit in the orchard, carefully hidden between the houses on the streets of 12th Avenue. I am raised by the Black Panthers, Y2K, and by ancestors who lived through the depression: longshoremen, teamsters, business owners, home owners, and housemaids.

I am a strategist, creative, seamstress, quilter, embroiderer, book enthusiast, collector of stories and things, and an advocate for the simple life.

I am a pedagogical leader, a gate-opener, a system changer, a provocateur, and a change agent.

PLANTED

I am Kelly Sanders Ramsey.

I began my journey in this field over thirty-five years ago, as a high school graduate taking a summer job at Jardin Montessori School in Berkeley, California. I was a teacher's aide. In my mind that meant clearing tables, taking children to the restroom, and patting backs at naptime. The owner of the Montessori school, which was housed in two Victorian homes, had a new idea for the role of teacher's assistant. I was immersed in learning about Montessori classrooms, seeing children as creators of their own learning, and learning how observation tells us what to offer next, to the child who is learning from the world around them. It was a great beginning that has framed my work from that day forward.

I consider every experience a pebble in my garden, which formed as I shifted spaces and contributed my entire self to the space. My next journey would take me to Southern California as a preschool teacher for a private child care center, where I met children who changed my approach to setting up environments. This experience offered me the support of a co-teacher, and I learned what it meant to work as a team, share ideas, and create and reconfigure environments. In this space, the outdoor classroom offered children choice and the opportunity to explore.

My learning was a parallel process with the children, as we figured things out together. I was a student at Chabot Community College in Hayward, and wanted to take every lesson and explore how it would fit in my classroom. My excitement led to me change things weekly, and my co-teacher gently reminded me that the children were overwhelmed and needed consistent environments to support their learning. When a child echoed the thoughts of my colleague by asking me, "Teacher, where did you put the block area?" I heard her loud and clear. In my experience as a teacher, that's what I felt like too. I was learning and growing, yet the environments to support my own learning kept "moving the block areas." This led me to seek my own path and make my own blocks. The path always led me to the work of Deb Curtis and Margie Carter, which gave me a foundation to expand my reflective practice as a teacher.

The blocks represented for me innovation, resourcefulness, creativity, and necessity. I had no materials, so I built what I needed and used them until they no longer were needed. Never discarding them, but passing them on to the next teacher who was just starting out. At that time, I had two crates of teacher resource books to help me create lesson plans and learning materials. The crates moved with me to my next destination, Pasadena, and more opportunities to seek out models to promote social justice, equity and inclusion.

For this leg of my journey there would be no guide, so I would draw on the years at Jardin Montessori School, make and take conferences, and my introduction to NAEYC resources and colleagues. In my journey, I always wanted a mentor to guide my practice and provide insight on ideas I had, to really serve families and children. When the teacher didn't appear I sought out my own. I took a risk to attach to work that was going on at Pacific Oaks College, related to the anti-bias book that Louise Derman Sparks had just

> "I REALIZED THAT IN ORDER TO SERVE CHILDREN, I MUST PARTNER WITH FAMILIES AND LEARN FROM THEM."
>
> — KELLY RAMSEY

written. I devoured the pages and made it a part of my children's experience in class, and used it to bridge what families bring to a program beyond the open house snacks and monthly treat for the children.

It was at this point that I realized in order to serve children, I must partner with families and learn from them. My books gave me ideas, but now I was moving to places where reflection and dialogue were needed, to propel programs forward. I started to create a library of reflective practices. I sought conferences that would nurture the idea that we are co-contributors to learning, when learning is a collaborative process. The settings I worked in were traditional child care programs, but my classrooms and thoughts transcended the traditional and dared to take risks and test boundaries.

My journey returned me to my own childhood and parents, who allowed me space, time, and experiences to learn through and grow. This foundation supported the experiences I offered to children and families, and helped me to establish my own philosophy rooted in the resilience of families. As educators, we are in a place to always acknowledge the families as they come to us. We acknowledge their strength, respect their beliefs, treat them with dignity, and most importantly partner with them in their journey to give their children experiences that are rich, filled with wonder and creative adventures.

This is the same goal for educators; we can't provide for families what we are unwilling to experience ourselves. This revelation opened up new training opportunities to explore with teachers, and my desire to introduce a new way of thinking about the early childhood classroom. The question I posed was,

"What if we treated educators as we require them to treat children? What if we treated them with respect, providing opportunity for exploration and discovery, partnering with them in inquiry, pausing and waiting for thinking, accepting ideas and input?"

My journey is unique because I sought connections to strengthen my role as an ECE leader. In that search I encountered many closed doors because of my reflective nature and desire to create a more equitable practice for all educators, regardless of culture or background. I began to imagine a system that would engage all educators respectfully and authentically. I created communities of practice to demonstrate what it feels like to be listened to fully, to offer ideas and have them welcomed, and to create space for provocations that took us away from just staying within the walls of our work to busting out the walls and building windows that shift paradigms for lifelong learning.

In the space of my two-year-old classrooms, I began to understand that our work as educators transcends the walls of our classroom. As I was experiencing this revelation, my center director was looking to cultivate leadership in me. I pushed back. I was afraid to risk change and enter into the unknown expectations of a leader. She exposed me to the local work of committees focused on sharing progressive ideas on children's environments and curriculum. This invitation to join her for an experience working alongside educators in Southern California would offer me space to learn with other leaders committed to worthy wages, quality learning for young children, and systems that support all educators. In a few short years, she would leave the child care center and I would become the director of Glendale Childcare Consortium.

KELLY RAMSEY

As a center director, my heart was grounded in the classroom and focused on what an educator needed to fully attend to children's learning and development. I thought of all the things I needed as a teacher and sought to provide them. The space to talk about our work, materials to use and explore with children, acknowledgement of the work in the classroom, and space to breathe and take a break were all elements that I had the power to create with and for educators in my center. At this phase of my career, there emerged another book from Margie and Deb: "The Visionary Director." Margie and Deb continued to inspire me through their work. "The Visionary Director" would become my guide for the next decade, as I moved from Southern California to Oklahoma to continue my journey. I still had my crates in tow, but a growing library of reflective practice books was starting to form.

The journey to Oklahoma left me with a space to decide how I wanted to begin again. My career in California had given me roots in my practice and a great foundation of experiences to share with teachers in Oklahoma. I enrolled in college and completed my bachelor's and master's degrees during this time. This positioned me to become an adjunct teacher for the community college. The role of adjunct provided space to grow teachers in a brand new way. As I worked in my program, I had concrete examples of how we were transforming environments and creating collaborative spaces for teachers and children. Sharing the stories of the work and providing a new paradigm for teachers pursuing their degree were daily highlights of my practice.

In sharing those practices, I became aware that taking a risk is scary and not all environments are equitable. This presented the idea of who gets to come to the table when opportunity presents itself. As a leader in education, I was invited to the table to represent the programs where I had a sphere of influence. At the table, I was Kelly, education manager for Head Start. I was Kelly Ramsey, daughter of Albert and Linda Sanders. When I come to the table, this is what I bring. Always remembering that I represent all who came before me—my ancestors, and those I serve in my programs and communities, and most importantly my authentic self.

The idea of joining a table by invitation or pulling up a chair to a table to offer yourself, has resonated in my journey. This places us in a space to contribute to the dialogue that is forming. We establish our voice and assist in framing the direction of our work. I would like to believe that in this season of my work as a leader, I have the capacity to hold both what is available and what is yet to be. I am at the helm of opportunity to create a new table with other like-minded individuals who believe that all voices matter and all individuals deserve a space. When there is not a table available, we get to decide how to start a conversation, who to invite, and how we engage meaningfully. By nature, I am a teacher. Always learning alongside others and creating disequilibrium in our practices to offer a new perspective. In the words of a dear friend, "This is the space where magic happens." So, join me at the table, as we open up possibilities for educators to explore and learn together.

KELLY RAMSEY

Kelly Ramsey is a passionate teacher, focused visionary, and a purpose-driven leader. As the owner of Developing People, Inc., Kelly fosters engaging learning environments that help individuals to discover the greatness within. She believes that everyone was created with a purpose, and we are on a journey to figure out just what that purpose is. Her work has expanded to building communities through individual consulting, We-Connect Communities and capacity building with non-profit agencies.

REFLECTION QUESTIONS

1 Kelly shares her legacy and ancestry with us in her story. Why is it important to understand where you come from when you are preparing to bring your voice to the table?

2 The road to leadership was long for Kelly. What factors helped change the trajectory of her career?

3 If your dream is leadership, what lessons could you take from Kelly's story to help you get there? If you are already a leader, what could you do to bring forth new voices?

"... I STOPPED CARING WHAT OTHER PEOPLE THOUGHT I WAS CAPABLE OF AND STARTED FOCUSING ON WHAT I WANTED TO DO."

— ALISSA MWENELUPEMBE

RESILIENCE
ALISSA MWENELUPEMBE

When I was eight years old, a boy in my second grade classroom told me I was Black. I didn't know what he meant, but his tone told me it was something I should be ashamed of. I grew up living with my mom, my grandparents, and a variety of aunts and uncles; all white. In some ways I knew that I was different from them. My aunts would often comment in the summer how they wanted to turn brown like me, well not all of me, just the lightest parts. And doing my hair often seemed to be the source of distress. My grandpa had an olive complexion and jet black hair on his head and arms, so my child's brain rationalized that he and I were the same. So, that day when that child told me I was Black, I mostly felt confused. Looking back on this experience as an adult, I know that the confusion I felt was also mixed with shame that continued to follow me throughout my childhood and into adolescence.

After eight years at an all white (except me) very small, Catholic school I moved on to public high school. My high school was definitely more diverse than my grade school had been, but still very segregated. I only had experience interacting with white students, so I found myself continuing to be in white friend circles, but always curious about my Black peers. I was stuck between two worlds: not white, so never truly fitting in with my white friends, and culturally different from potential Black friends. I went all through high school longing to fit and feeling too ashamed to share that longing with anyone.

The realities of racism started to become clearer to me in high school. In grade school it was not rare that some of the kids would lump my skin color in with their bullying, but I always felt supported by the adults in the school. In high school I had my first experience with a teacher who exhibited racist actions. In my sophomore English class I was the only Black student. I loved English and it had always been my favorite subject. I was also an excellent student and rarely caused trouble in class. The teacher regularly disciplined me for reasons that I could never understand. I was always being called out. I had developed a close bond with my freshman English teacher. I did really well in her class the previous year and felt safe with her. I went to her to try to get some advice on what I could be doing differently in my class to avoid getting in trouble every day. Mrs. Alcorn told me that I wasn't doing anything wrong. She rocked my world when she said that my teacher didn't like Black students and nothing I could do would make her treat me differently. As a fifteen-year-old who had never had a real conversation about race in her life, I was stunned. Her advice to me was to complain to the principal and get moved to a different class. I was thankful that my mom took this advice seriously and helped me get moved to a class where I not only wasn't the only Black student, but also a class where I was able to shine.

It wasn't until college that I began to make real connections with Black students. I went to a university in my home town which was in many ways an extension of my high school, but I did get the chance to meet students from other places. As we got older our interactions branched out to bars and clubs where I encountered new people and expanded my circle. My university was still quite white and the English department where I completed my undergrad coursework was extremely white. I had my first Black teacher during this time. Dr. Betty Hart was fierce and refused to take any bullshit from any of her students and especially her Black ones. While I found so much joy in all of my English courses, I felt especially seen in hers. While she was pushing for Black excellence in her African American literature course, I was having different experiences in other courses that I took. I felt really connected to another professor at the university, a white woman. I took six courses with her throughout my degree program. She was an excellent teacher, but the day I suggested that I might want to go on to do my master's and then my doctorate she immediately persuaded me against it and said she didn't think that it was for me. I trusted her and at that moment I shut the door on an advanced degree in an area that I loved so very much. I assumed that after six classes together (that I mostly received As in for the record) that she knew that my work wasn't up to par. I trusted her to help me make an important life decision. A few years after graduation I stopped by the university to say hello to my professors. She seemed to barely know who I was (remember six classes I took with her). At that point I realized that her judgment of my future success in graduate school probably didn't have very much to do with my academic achievements at all. I look forward to reaching out to her in the future so that I have the opportunity to sign my name Dr. Alissa Mwenelupembe.

As I moved into my adult life, I still struggled with my identity. In my hometown it seemed there was a certain way to be Black and I didn't fit. I was told by people that I met (Black folks) that I "didn't act Black" or that I "talked white." There were so many times that I wished I could change who I was so I could fit, not unlike the eight-year-old little girl who just wanted to fit in with her classmates. But, at the same time, I felt this pressure from my white family to not change and to "be like us." I was even extremely careful about introducing the guys that I dated based on how I thought my family would react to them. I met my husband when I was twenty-two years old. He is African and it seemed that his foreign-ness would be more acceptable to my family and cancel out his Blackness. I was probably right about that. For my whole life I had been navigating race, but never actually talking about it. I had to move away from the comfort of my family to start to feel comfortable in my own skin.

After five years of marriage and two children, my husband Sekela and I moved away from my hometown of Evansville, Indiana to Louisville, Kentucky. Our hope was that a larger city would be more diverse and give us more opportunities as well as offer our kids more opportunity to be around Black folks. There, in my early childhood center, I had my first experience of being accepted as a Black person. In some ways I was different from my staff, but they chalked it up to the fact that I wasn't from there, not that I acted white. They embraced

> "I HAD TO MOVE AWAY FROM THE COMFORT OF MY FAMILY TO START TO FEEL COMFORTABLE IN MY OWN SKIN."
>
> — ALISSA MWENELUPEMBE

RESILIENCE

me as "Alissa" and I began to feel like I had a community. Their support began to help me find my voice. I got bolder and called out the unfairness that I saw happening all around me. I stood up to those who tried to keep the community surrounding my center down, and I raised my hand when I felt that I deserved an opportunity. During this time I began to learn more about social justice issues and connected with people from all over the country that were doing this work in early childhood education. I also began to connect with national early childhood organizations through volunteer opportunities. I always knew that I had potential but I was never sure anyone else agreed. During those years in Louisville I stopped caring what other people thought I was capable of and started focusing on what I wanted to do. It was during those years that, like the Shirley Chisolm quote that Kelly Ramsey shared with me years later stated, I always brought my folding chair.

While I found my voice and power amongst my staff in Louisville, there were many people who planted the seeds along the way. My grandma was an essential person in my life from day one. While my white grandma couldn't teach me one thing about being Black, she taught me a lot about being a woman who uses her voice. My grandma had an eighth grade education, fourteen children and only worked outside of her home once in her life, but she had a strong voice and it was evident that she made the decisions in her house, even though she would always say she had to check with my grandpa before agreeing to anything. She cared for me so deeply and fully that I always felt seen with her and I always felt like I was a special person who deserved to be seen. That was important to me growing up because I didn't always feel that way in my own house. She was always my soft place to land. We never talked about race when I was growing up, but we often did when I became an adult, especially after my kids were born. I don't feel like she ever claimed to understand my experiences but she listened and she paid attention. When my daughter was little she always made a point to give her Black dolls and not only did she buy them for Maya, she bought them for her other great-granddaughters too, even the white ones. One year she gifted my family with a Black Santa and Mrs. Claus statue. We rolled our eyes a little at the time because it was kind of a corny gift, but that statue still sits on my shelf every Christmas. When she died in 2020 I thought a lot about all that she had seen in her lifetime and how the world had changed. While some older white people spend their time digging in their heels, my grandma was willing to course correct and go down a different path. I know that I wouldn't be who I am today without her care and support and I miss her every day.

"WHILE SOME OLDER WHITE PEOPLE SPEND THEIR TIME DIGGING IN THEIR HEELS, MY GRANDMA WAS WILLING TO COURSE CORRECT AND GO DOWN A DIFFERENT PATH. I KNOW THAT I WOULDN'T BE WHO I AM TODAY WITHOUT HER CARE AND SUPPORT AND I MISS HER EVERY DAY."

— ALISSA MWENELUPEMBE

"If they don't give you a seat at the table, bring a folding chair." Shirley Chisolm, a woman that I never knew and had never heard of until I was an adult, spoke of the thing that I have been finding myself doing my whole life. As a child I lived in an in-between space. I wasn't white enough to fit with the white folks, not Black enough to feel at home with the Black folks. I never felt invited to any tables, but I kept showing up. I took that same thing into my adult life as I navigated my career. Who were my mentors? Who lived the way I hoped to live that I could look to and learn from? So, I kept finding my seat at tables. Sometimes invited, other times because I carried my hypothetical folding chair on my back. I would notice the meeting where important decisions were being made and I would figure out how to find my way there. One of my favorite examples of my expert ability to find my seat happened when I was a young trainer and coach in my local CCR&R. I had been reading the work of Margie Carter and Deb Curtis and leading a group of directors in a study of, "The Visionary Director." I saw that Margie would be leading a two-day pre-conference institute at the McCormick Leadership Connections conference. I found a way to fund my trip through a grant and found myself at a table in the institute. I went alone and did not know a single person there, but found myself the first night at dinner with Margie and the facilitators of the institute. I found my literal seat at the table at a Mexican restaurant with a group of people who both intimidated and inspired me. I knew that I wanted to be at that table again. Flash forward about four years and I found myself at another table with Margie Carter. This one in Louisville, Kentucky where I found myself as a facilitator at a Harvest Resources Institute. Remember that table at the Mexican restaurant with Margie and the facilitators? From that deeper connection with the Harvest Resources Associates I knew that was the next table I wanted to find myself at. After a couple of years serving as an institute facilitator, I was officially invited to join Harvest Resources as an associate.

So, what does it mean for a little girl who grew up not even knowing she was Black to find herself in a position to elevate the voices of Black women? I think about that every day. I believe that's part of the reason why I've been able to find my seat at the table is because of the whiteness that I experienced as a child. For many years I relied heavily on the privilege that I acquired because of that whiteness. In my thirties it began to feel more like a burden than a privilege and I started to feel embarrassed. Was I upholding the systems of white supremacy instead of working to dismantle them? Was I acting like a safe Black person instead of pushing for full inclusivity? In reality I was just operating in the systems that I knew and feeling ashamed was not helpful. As I move into my forties I'm starting to live in a space where many things can be true. Yes, I have a lot of experience with whiteness and I navigate in white spaces well. How can I use that as a platform to elevate my Black colleagues instead of feeling guilty or like a sellout? How can I use the tools that I was given to infiltrate and educate? I'm still asking myself these questions every day and considering what the possibilities are for myself, my Black children, and my community.

"I NEVER FELT INVITED
TO ANY TABLES,
BUT I KEPT SHOWING UP."

— ALISSA MWENELUPEMBE

ALISSA MWENELUPEMBE

Alissa Mwenelupembe has spent the last twenty years navigating her space to find her seat at the table. Alissa started her career in early childhood education as an assistant teacher in a two-year-old classroom. Since that time she has held the roles of teacher, director, coach/mentor, content specialist, and now leads the early learning accreditation system for the National Association for the Education of Young Children. Alissa is a passionate advocate for young children, their families, and their educators. She is currently pursuing her doctorate in early childhood education at Ball State University.

REFLECTION QUESTIONS

1 What is your earliest memory of race or skin color?

2 Alissa's upbringing included a combination of racial and cultural settings, yet she did not feel belonging. What brought her to start to step into her own space, rather than what was outlined for her?

3 Where are places you have felt belonging, kinship, and safety? Are they related to your roles and identities? How can you create safe spaces for others?

"IT'S MY HOPE THAT THIS COLLECTION MIGHT INSPIRE YOU TO BECOME CURIOUS ABOUT THE STORIES OF THE PEOPLE AROUND YOU."

— ALISSA MWENELUPEMBE

AFTERWORD

One time, I was in a job interview for a director level position. A white man, commenting on what he saw was my lack of leadership experience, stated that his last three jobs had been in state level leadership, yet I had none. My stomach dropped and the tears immediately sprang to my eyes. So many thoughts came to my head in the moment that it took for me to respond. I wanted to say,

"My mom works at a grocery store; do you think she knew to give me the guidance to start doing internships my senior year of undergrad so that I could land a state level job after graduation? Even if I had known that things like internships were important, I worked in college so that I could eat and have a bed to sleep in at night. No one was paying for me to be comfortable while I got my education. Even today, I do not have the luxury to move to our capital to try to get a job that may not even exist."

More than anything, it hurt me that his assumption was that I never even tried. That it was so easy for him to have gotten where he was today that he could not even conceive why someone else was not there also.

My experience growing up was so very different from the others that you read in this book. The other authors talked about having strong role models that helped them understand what it meant to be a Black woman in

America. I often long for that sort of education. My family loved me a lot, and they could teach me many things, but they couldn't teach me anything about being Black, because they were all white. I grew up carrying the pain of being different and feeling othered, not because they told me that my Blackness was bad, but because we never talked about it at all.

In my family we called my skin "brown," and we never talked about why it was like that. It just was. I knew I had a dad out in the world somewhere, but we also didn't talk about him. When we didn't talk about these things, my child brain started assuming that they must be taboo (although I'm certain I didn't know that word). I went on through my childhood and adolescent years trying to figure out what it meant to be a Black woman and looking for role models along the way.

> "WHEN I READ THE STORIES IN THIS BOOK FOR THE FIRST TIME, I WAS REMINDED OF HOW NO TWO STORIES ARE THE SAME, YET THEY ALL HAVE VALUE."
>
> — ALISSA MWENELUPEMBE

Now, at thirty-eight years old, I have found connections with many women who have helped me to see myself and figure out where I fit. When I read the stories in this book for the first time, I was reminded of how no two stories are the same, yet they all have value. For many years, I carried the shame of not fitting into one category completely. As an adult, I have been able to let go of that shame and embrace myself exactly as I am. I can see myself in the little girl from Brandy's story who knows that she doesn't fit in, but isn't exactly sure how. I can see myself in Nadiyah, who looks so closely at the world and studies how it works and never apologizes for her brilliant brain. I can see myself in Kelly, whose words are like poetry and tell the story of a woman who has spent her life studying the system so she knows it well enough to navigate her way in and then reroute it completely. I see myself in all of these women, because I am a part of this community. Each author in this collection shared a word that they believed captured their story, and it felt important to choose a word of my own. When I reflected on my journey with its ups and downs and highs and lows the only word that felt right is resilient. We are not where we come from and we are not what has happened to us. We can choose our future, so I keep getting back up and moving forward.

It's my hope that this collection might inspire you to become curious about the stories of the people around you. I hope that you don't just start to wonder about each other, but begin a dialogue through which you can find out things you never imagined. One in which you can see both your similarities and your differences. Where you can truly start to see each other. And then, when you have the opportunity, you can find ways to elevate the stories of those around you who might not have the power to do so themselves.

Toni Morrison, who happens to be my favorite author, once said, "If there is a book that you want to read, but it hasn't been written yet, then you must write it."

This was a book that I wanted to read when I was a little girl with brown skin, surrounded by a sea of white faces, wondering where I fit. I wanted to read this book when I went to college and spent four years at a university, but was only taught by one Black professor. I wanted to read this book when I brought another little brown girl into this world and held my breath as she navigated the world, looking for faces that resembled hers. And today, I still want to read this book, because Black voices are being silenced through senseless acts of violence and racism and I know that the only way we can move forward is to keep sharing stories just like these.

Thank you for taking the first step forward.

— Alissa Mwenelupembe

www.ingramcontent.com/pod-product-compliance
Lightning Source LLC
Chambersburg PA
CBHW061258170426
43191CB00042B/2456